COVENANT, CHARTER, A

COVENANT, CHARTER, AND PARTY

Traditions of revolt and protest
in modern Scottish History

edited by
Terry Brotherstone

ABERDEEN UNIVERSITY PRESS

First published 1989
Aberdeen University Press
A member of the Maxwell Pergamon Macmillan Group
© The contributors 1989

British Library Cataloguing in Publication Data

Covenant, charter and party: traditions of revolt and
protest in modern Scottish history.
1. Scotland. Protest movements, history
I. Brotherstone, Terry
322.4′4′09411

ISBN 0 08 037736 X

Typeset from author generated discs
and printed by AUP Glasgow/Aberdeen—A member of BPCC Ltd.

In Memory
Julie Macwhirter
(1944-1981)

CONTENTS

LIST OF CONTRIBUTORS

TERRY BROTHERSTONE is Lecturer in History at the University of Aberdeen
ROGER MASON is Lecturer in Scottish History at the University of St Andrews
V.G. KIERNAN is Emeritus Professor of History at the University of Edinburgh
JOHN BRIMS is Glenfiddich Research Fellow in Scottish History at the University of St Andrews
W. HAMISH FRASER is Senior Lecturer in History at the University of Strathclyde
ROBERT DUNCAN is Tutor-Organiser for Lanarkshire Workers' Educational Association
WILLIAM KNOX is Lecturer in Economic and Social History at the University of St Andrews

PREFACE

Between November 1987 and March 1988 the Centre for Scottish Studies held a series of six seminars to commemorate simultaneously the 350th anniversary of the first signing, in Edinburgh, of the National Covenant, and the 150th anniversary of the first major Chartist demonstration, which took place in Glasgow. The intention was not to suggest that there was any direct link between the two events, but to use the coincidence of these two anniversaries to explore a number of themes relating to protest and rebellion in Scotland since the seventeenth century, whether direct links between them can be traced or not. The result was a very interesting and lively series of meetings. The seminars were organised by my colleague Terry Brotherstone, and he has now edited the papers for publication (as we decided that they were of more than ephemeral value), and has added an introduction, a short essay, and some concluding comments reflecting on points made during the seminar discussions.

DAVID STEVENSON
Director of the Centre for Scottish Studies
and Reader in Scottish History
University of Aberdeen

EDITOR'S NOTE

In February 1638, the Scottish National Covenant was first signed at Grey-friars churchyard in Edinburgh—a key link in a chain of events which led to the execution of Charles I and Britain's only experiment so far with a republic. Two hundred years later, in May 1838, the chartists—pioneers of working-class politics in Britain—held their first national demonstration in Glasgow. Eighty years after that, in December 1918, the first of the 'Red Clydesiders' was elected to parliament, a harbinger of the Independent Labour Party's sensational election success in Glasgow in 1922, and of the advent of the first Labour government in 1924.

Taking the 350th anniversary of the Covenant and the 150th anniversary of the Charter as a stimulus, the Centre for Scottish Studies at the University of Aberdeen held a series of seminars during 1987-88. The idea was to examine occasions of revolt and protest in Scottish history, and perhaps to explore whether studying the covenanters, chartists and Clydesiders side-by-side might highlight continuities and differences in the history of mass movements of political opposition to authority in Scotland.

The six seminar papers—along with some additional comments by the editor—are now published in *Covenant, Charter, and Party*. They combine scholarship and analysis with a consciousness of the need to communicate with a growing audience drawn to the study of Scottish history by the mounting evidence in the 1980s that, even after nearly three hundred years of union, the northern part of the kingdom has not entirely lost its separate political traditions.

Five of the essays are by scholars with established—or rapidly being estab-lished—reputations as specialists in particular aspects of Scottish history. The sixth is Professor V.G. Kiernan, the 'British Marxist historian', who, although better known for his work on imperialism and many other subjects, is one of the most celebrated writers of history to have worked in Scotland since the Second World War.

INTRODUCTION

They were '... funny chaps the Covenanters, he had always liked them', the young communist Ewan Tavendale told his girl-friend in Lewis Grassic Gibbon's novel of the early 1930s, *Grey Granite*. And he went on to call them 'the advance guard of the common folk of those days, their God and their Covenant just formulae they hid the social rebellion in'. Reflecting on his own recent experiences at the hands of the Scottish police, he recalled the time when 'the gentry' imprisoned and killed covenanters 'in scores'.

> ... And his face grew dark, no boy's face: *There's nothing new under the sun—not even torture.*[1]

In a letter to *The Scotsman* newspaper in the autumn of 1988, a correspondent, expressing ironic approval for a nationalist critic who had queried whether Scotland's leading opera, ballet and orchestral bodies could legitimately be cited as examples of a thriving *Scottish* culture, compared him to C.M. Grieve (the poet, Hugh MacDiarmid). Grieve, said the letter-writer, had once attacked Sir Donald Tovey, a world-renowned expert on the concerto, for his neglect of the music of his native Scotland. The poet cared nothing for Tovey's achievements nor his world-wide reputation, the letter claimed, because his (Grieve's)

> was the spirit which animated the Covenanting remnant of the 1680s, who, although harried from pillar to post by the dragoons, did not hesitate to excommunicate the king.

And the letter concluded:

> This spirit is still alive in the nationalists of today. We must be grateful for the existence of men who are prepared to defy the stars in their courses; the world would not be the same without them.[2]

The 'advanced guard of the common folk'; or 'men who are prepared to defy the stars in their courses': which, if either, were the covenanters? Are both images *purely* subjective, or does each express a real truth about different aspects of covenanting history? In chapter I of this volume Roger Mason tells of the formation, in the late 1630s, of a political alliance between part of the

1

Scottish landed elite, with a feudal social outlook, and a group of clerical ideologues, which on the one hand, may seem to be historically unique, leading, as it did, to the 'English revolution' of the 1640s; and, on the other, to find at least an echo in events as recent as the Iranian revolution of 1979. In chapter II Victor Kiernan analyses the process by which this alliance dissolved into 'the covenanting remnant' of the Restoration years. What is it about this story of failure which made it hauntingly attractive to a young Scottish communist in the 1930s, and polemically useful to our more recent exemplar of the 'Dear editor' brigade? Furthermore, given the evident capacity of the covenanters to create some sort of stirring image in the minds of twentieth century Scots, by what lineage of revolt, if any, are we today linked with the rebels of the seventeenth century? Are the covenanters merely providers of good yarns of men and women of dogged courage to be picked up at random by people with concerns as various as socialist revolution and the work of Scottish Opera; or is it possible to begin to uncover a tradition of subversive ideology (or even of forms of struggle), drawing on the covenanting past and giving its meaning a new content in battles against new enemies? Did the covenanting ideal inspire the Scottish radicalism of the era of the French Revolution, aspects of which are analysed by John Brims in chapter III? Did it play any part in the efforts of the men and women who rallied to the cause of the People's Charter in Scotland in the late 1830s, different facets of which are discussed by Hamish Fraser and Robert Duncan in chapters IV and V? And, if Leslie Mitchell (Lewis Grassic Gibbon), at a time when Stalin was consolidating his perverted grip on the world communist movement, could make his communist character Ewan animadvert on a Scottish hillside about the covenanters, what impact did the covenanting tradition have on that much more obviously popular socialist movement in interwar Scotland, the Independent Labour Party (ILP)? William Knox refers to this question in chapter VI.

These questions give some hint of the subterranean theme flowing unobtrusively beneath the surface of the contributions to this volume. But the individual chapters do not follow any pre-charted course. The lecture/seminars from which the book derives were organised by the Centre for Scottish Studies at the University of Aberdeen over the winter of 1987-88. The pretext for the subjects chosen was that 28 February 1988 was the 350th anniversary of the first signings of the National Covenant at Greyfriars Church in Edinburgh; and 28 May of the same year was the 150th anniversary of the first mass chartist demonstration in Britain, held in Glasgow in 1838.[3]

Aberdeen, sometimes seen as a conservative centre at times when other Scottish cities have been focal points for political radicalism or intellectual dissent, provided a good vantage point from which to survey some key moments of revolt, or at least substantial protest, in modern Scottish history. To be doing so in Aberdeen's almost 500 year-old university seemed, at least to me, particularly poignant, since, in the last decade, members of that rather conservative of professions, university teaching, in this usually rather conservative city, sometimes found themselves responding to a policy of public economy by seeking a language of, and ways of organising, protest, though not quite revolt.[4]

The furtherance of present day protest, however, was no part of the purpose of the seminars. Indeed if any common outlook—historical or political—beyond a respect for evidence and a conviction about the importance of historical discourse, were to inform the essays which follow, it would be entirely coincidental. The contributors were invited on the grounds of their scholarly reputations, and their current interest in the particular fields chosen for the series;[5] and there was no opportunity for collective discussion. The seminars took place a minimum of a week apart over a period of almost three months, and the distance between Aberdeen and St Andrews, Stow, Glasgow, Motherwell and Edinburgh, where the contributors were severally based, made it impossible for any one of them to come and hear any of the other papers.

The value to which this volume aspires, therefore, does not lie in any collective argument. It is based, on the one hand, on the virtues—which to me seem both manifest and manifold—of the individual chapters; and, on the other, on the questions which may be prompted by the perhaps rather unusual juxtaposition of topics. The desire to prompt new questions—or maybe only the asking of old ones in new ways—must serve as excuse for including two chapters on different aspects of 'Red Clydeside' during the First World War and the 1920s, for no special anniversary was being recognised in this regard; although, for the fastidious, it might be observed that 28 December 1988 was seventy years since the declaration of the election of the first of the 'wild men' from the Clyde to the taming debating chamber by the Thames.[6]

If a diversity of outlook is detectable in what follows, it will also be noted that no editorial uniformity has been imposed with regard to scholarly apparatus. On reflection, to try to do so seemed both unreasonable and impossible, given that each essay—while they all have something to say both to specialists and non-specialists—has its own presentational logic. Drs Mason and Knox provided manuscripts with about the number of footnotes I had originally thought desirable; but it would have violated Dr Brims' scholarship to have placed his references upon a Procrustean bed of their, and my, making. I was more ruthless with Professor Kiernan, feeling that his scholarly reputation was too well-established to be damaged by editorial arrogance on my part; but I am fairly confident that readers will suffer no major inconvenience from the compression (with his permission) of his original one hundred and twelve footnotes down to seventy.

In compensation for lopping a limb or two from Professor Kiernan, I have stretched out Dr Fraser and Mr Duncan to the extent of providing what seemed to me essential references where they—quite properly awaiting further instructions—provided none. The nature of the volume seemed to justify this authoritarianism (again with their permission) but it should be made clear that I bear the main responsibility for any errors in the references to chapters IV and V. Since the nature of Mr Duncan's piece necessitated only one or two notes apart from reference to his own other work, I asked him to provide a short reading list on chartism which will also be relevant to pursuers of points made by Dr Fraser. This is at p.91. A comparable list on the covenanters, by Dr Mason, appears at pp.23-4.

It remains only to thank all the contributors; David Stevenson, the indefatigably efficient director of the Centre for Scottish Studies; everyone who attended and thereby contributed, whether questioningly or mutely, to the success of the seminars; Mr Colin MacLean and Miss Moira Harper of Aberdeen University Press; and, above all, Mrs Margaret Croll of the Centre for Scottish Studies without whose expertise on the word processor and patience with my erratic typing, antique lapses into handwriting, and eccentric proofreading, you would not be reading this book at all. May whatever virtues the volume has redound to the credit of them all. Its failings will—no doubt very properly—be placed squarely on my shoulders.

Terry Brotherstone,
30 March 1989

NOTES

1. Lewis Grassic Gibbon, *A Scots Quair* (Harmondsworth, 1986) 464. (*Grey Granite*, the final volume of the trilogy was first published in 1934).
2. *The Scotsman*, 21 October 1988.
3. 'Glasgow was the first place of any considerable note to make a grand and effective display of the attachment of its citizens to the rising movement, and there ensued such a display as will never be forgotten, by those who witnessed the proceedings'. R.G. Gammage, *History of the Chartist Movement, 1837-1854* (Newcastle-on-Tyne, 1894), 19-20.
4. See *Universities against the Cuts*, ed. T. Brotherstone and J.A. Hook, (Aberdeen, 1982).
5. Professor Kiernan's best-known research interests, of course, have not lain in Scottish history. I asked him to contribute because I knew of his longstanding interest in the country he adopted after the Second World War, which up until recently has surfaced mainly in his less 'official' writings. As he is one of the best-known internationally of professional historians working in Scotland over the better part of the last half-century, this was an appropriate moment to ask him to rub shoulders, in a literary sense, with a number of Scottish experts on Scotland. It also seems to me that a notable gap in the *opera* of that influential group of writers, dubbed, by the American social scientist, Harvey Kaye, 'the British Marxist historians', has been Scottish history. This is not said out of patriotic or parochial pique but out of the conviction—very much re-inforced by preparing the present volume—that there can be no overall understanding of *English* history which does not take fully into account the significance of the processes of integration which composed, but have never entirely harmonised, the United Kingdom.

   For Kiernan on Scotland, see, e.g. 'The Scottish Revolution...' in *Scottish Marxist*, (8 January 1975), 31-8; 'A Scottish Road to Socialism?', *New Left Review*, 93 (September-October, 1975), 93-114; 'The Covenanters: a Problem of Creed and Class', in *History from below: studies in popular protest and popular ideology in honour of George Rudé* ed. Frederick Krantz (Montreal, 1985), 95-124; or 53-82 in the English edition (Oxford, 1988).

   Kiernan and Rudé were largely omitted from Harvey Kaye's original analysis of *The British Marxist Historians* (Cambridge, 1984); but Kaye's rectification of this misjudgement may be found in his currently appearing editions of their collected essays. The first Kiernan volume is *History, Classes and Nation States* ed. H. Kaye (Cambridge, 1988).

   Other excursions by 'the British Marxist historians' into Scottish history include E.J. Hobsbawm, 'The Other Britain', chapter 15 of his *Industry and Empire* (Harmondsworth, 1969); and the same author's 'Scottish Reformers of the Eighteenth Century and Capitalist Agriculture', in *Peasants in History...* ed. Hobsbawm *et al.* (Oxford, 1980). Hobsbawm's comments on tradition in *The Invention of Tradition* ed. Hobsbawm and Ranger (Cambridge, 1983), 1-14, may also stimulate thought about the themes of the present volume, though from a quite different angle. Attention to Scotland is confined to H.R. Trevor-Roper, 'The Invention of Tradition: the Highland Traditon of Scotland', *ibid.*, 15-41, and students of Highland history may find Trevor-Roper's reference to the *particular* Highland tradition he so wittily surveys as *the* Highland tradition, a trifle one-sided.
6. Neil Maclean (1873-1953) who was elected for Govan with a majority of 815. The result of the general election, held on 14 December 1918, was announced

on 28 December, Maclean, like the unrelated but more celebrated Marxist educator, and Bolshevik consul in Glasgow, John Maclean (1879-1923), had some Highland ancestry. Both, albeit indirectly, provide evidence of a Highland tradition different from Trevor-Roper's.

1 THE ARISTOCRACY, EPISCOPACY, AND THE REVOLUTION OF 1638[1]

Roger Mason

Late in 1638 the small but increasingly prosperous burgh of Glasgow witnessed one of the most momentous occasions in seventeenth-century Scottish history. For four weeks, between 21 November and 20 December, a large and motley crowd of notables packed into the nave of the town's ancient Cathedral and, after due deliberation, passed a series of measures which in effect amounted to a declaration of war against their lawful sovereign, King Charles I. Ostensibly an ecclesiastical gathering—the first General Assembly of the Church of Scotland to have met for twenty years—the Glasgow Assembly was in reality a gathering of those disaffected Scots—lay as well as clerical—whose opposition to the King's religious and political policies had led them earlier in the same year to subscribe the National Covenant. Indeed, it was during the Glasgow Assembly that so much that was only implicit in the National Covenant was made explicit and that a movement of protest and dissent was transformed into one of rebellion and revolution. It was the point of no return. Certainly, among the members of the Assembly few can have doubted that their deliberate defiance of the royal will—in particular their decision to abolish and abjure episcopacy—would lead to war against the King. Yet even the most prescient of the covenanters could hardly have foreseen that they were embarking on a course of action which would initiate a decade of civil strife—in Ireland and England as well as in Scotland—and lead ultimately to the abolition of the monarchy itself. Only with hindsight does it become clear that in 1638 Glasgow Cathedral was the scene of a decisive moment in the history of Charles I's unhappy relations with all three of his troubled kingdoms.

Although no previous occasion quite matches it in importance, 1638 was not in fact the first time that Glasgow had played host to a General Assembly of the kirk. Two contrasting but equally notable Assemblies had been held there in the past. The first occasion, in April 1581, had seen the ratification of both the Second Book of Discipline—Andrew Melville's visionary blueprint for a presbyterian Scotland—and the Negative or King's Confession—a rather less elevated attack on all things popish which was, significantly enough, to lie at the heart of the National Covenant of 1638. Just as important, though in complete contrast, it was another Assembly sitting in Glasgow in June 1610 which saw James VI & I finally realise his dream of taming the radical

7

presbyterians within the kirk through the full restoration of diocesan epis-copacy in Scotland. It was a victory long looked for, sorely won, but soon to be reversed in the reign of his son and successor. Had Charles I not sought to tamper with the ecclesiastical settlement hammered out by his father, the National Covenant would never have been drawn up and the Glasgow Assembly would never have met. As it was, the King's religious innovations provided the ideal focus for his Scottish subjects' profound distaste for the policies of their thoroughly anglicised monarch, while the Glasgow Assembly was to prove the ideal forum for the expression of their seething resentment and discontent.

Some sense of the excitement and apprehension stirred up by the Assembly is conveyed in the pages of Robert Baillie's incomparably informative *Letters and Journals*.[2] Baillie is one of those people whom it is hard to imagine being anything other than perpetually middle aged, but he was only in his mid thirties when the Assembly took place. Then minister of Kilwinning in Ayrshire, he was already betraying signs of that blend of censoriousness and pomposity which well suited him to his future career as a professor of divinity and which impart to his writings a uniquely comic flavour of which he himself was blissfully unaware. Here, for example, is his description of Glasgow in the heady days preceding the Assembly:

> The town did expect and provide for huge multitudes of people and put on their houses and beds excessive prices; but the diligence of the Magistrates, and the vacancy of many rooms, did quickly moderate that excess. We were glad to see such order and large provision above all men's expectation; for this that town got much both thanks and credit; it can lodge easily at once, both Council, Parliament, Session and General Assembly, whenever it shall be required.[3]

Not untouched by local patriotism, Baillie evidently thought that Glasgow could rival the capital city in its provision of conference facilities. This was probably not an opinion shared by Archibald Johnston of Wariston, the *angst*-ridden young advocate who, as a zealous adherent of the presbyterian cause, was to play a key role as clerk of the Assembly. Himself an Edinburgh man, Wariston lamented to God in his diary that, on arriving in Glasgow for the Assembly, he had had to waste a day's hard labour trudging 'from house to house seeking lodgings'.[4] He succeeded eventually in finding shared accom-modation for himself and two other prominent presbyterian figures. One of them was Alexander Henderson, minister of Leuchars in Fife, who was to be the Assembly's moderator and who, until his death in 1646, was to remain the covenanting movement's most astute and formidable religious leader. The other was the now ageing David Calderwood, an esteemed veteran whose knowledge of the early history of presbyterianism in Scotland was to prove as invaluable to the radicals in the Assembly as it is to the historians of today.

Both Baillie and Wariston provide eloquent testimony to the fact that Glasgow was bursting at the seams in November 1638 as people converged from all over Scotland to attend the Assembly. Baillie also supplies a uniquely detailed description of how this vast throng of people actually arranged themselves within the Cathedral. At the east end of the nave, he writes, sat the King's Commissioner, the Marquis of Hamilton, 'in his chair of state', and 'at his feet and on both sides' sat the chief members of the Privy Council. In addition,

> ... at a long table in the floor [sat] our noblemen and barons, elders of parishes, commissioners from presbyteries ... Few barons in Scotland of note, but were either voters or assessors; from every burgh, the chief burgess;... from all sixty-three presbyteries three commissioners, except a very few; from all the four universities also; sitting on good commodious rooms, rising up five or six degrees, going about the low long table. A little table was set in the midst, foreanent the Commissioner, for the Moderator and Clerk. At the end a high room prepared chiefly for young noblemen, ... with huge numbers of people, ladies, and some gentlewomen, in the vaults above.[5]

Quite clearly, this was no ordinary meeting of the General Assembly of the Church of Scotland. To be sure, no Assembly had been held since 1618 and there was some doubt—to which we will return later—as to who was entitled to attend. But the Assembly of 1638, packed with noblemen, lairds and burgesses as well as ministers, looks for all the world like a meeting of the three estates, a parliament representative of all the most powerful sections of Scottish society and dominated—as such a gathering would be—by the landed elite.

There is no room for doubt that this situation was deliberately engineered. As we will see, the elections to the Assembly were rigged not only to ensure that it was dominated by signatories of the National Covenant, but equally to ensure that the covenanters were themselves dominated by the lay leaders of Scottish society, the lairds and magnates. The appearance of social strength, respectability and unanimity was a matter of the first importance to the covenanters, for in reality their movement was never a wholly united, homogeneous organisation. It was an alliance, a coalition of disparate interests, a marriage of convenience between, principally, a cadre of presbyterian ministers and a group of disillusioned magnates. In time, of course, these interests were to diverge and ultimately the magnates were to fall victim to the ministers' radical vision of a godly society which was wholly at odds with their own conservative longings—idealised and distorted by nostalgia—for a past aristocratic order. But in 1638 the brittleness of the covenanter coalition was not yet apparent. As the Assembly approached, ministers and magnates were conscious only of the imperative need to maintain a united front in their opposition to the King. Besides, whatever their more deep-seated differences, superficially they did at least have one thing in common: a marked dislike of the episcopal bench and a mounting desire to limit—if not wholly to eliminate—its power and influence in the land.

The role of bishops in both church and state had been a matter of dispute in Scotland ever since the Reformation of 1560. There is no need here to rehearse the history of the long drawn out conflict between the proponents of episcopacy and their presbyterian opponents. Suffice it to say that, long before his death in 1625, James VI had won a resounding victory over the

Melvillians and established an erastian church in which royally appointed bishops played a dominant role in ecclesiastical administration. Critically, however, they were also employed as officers of state. While this caused few problems under the comparatively restrained and judicious governance of James VI, his son showed neither restraint nor good judgement. Unlike his father, Charles I was heavily influenced by the so-called Canterburian party within the Church of England led by the increasingly powerful Bishop (later Archbishop) William Laud. Drawn both by their Arminian theology—much less rigidly austere than orthodox Calvinism—and by their desire to adopt much more ceremonial liturgical practices, the King allowed Laud and his fellow Canterburians to assume a position of pre-eminent influence in both church and state. Generally speaking, the Scottish bishops—concerned to preserve the independence of the *Ecclesia Scoticana*—were much less Canterburian in their outlook than their English counterparts. Yet in Scotland too Charles I came to rely heavily on the episcopate in civil as well as in ecclesiastical administration. By the early 1630s bishops were sitting regularly and in increasing numbers on the privy council and—at least in the eyes of their enemies—were threatening to monopolise the ear of the King. The worst fears of the anti-episcopal lobby were apparently confirmed when in 1635 Charles elevated John Spottiswoode, Archbishop of St Andrews, to the chancellorship. Not since before the Reformation, since the heyday of the infamous Cardinal David Beaton, had a cleric held this, the highest office of state.

Under the circumstances it is perhaps not surprising that by 1638 the episcopate had become both the focus and symbol of all that was thought to be wrong with Charles I's government of Scotland. It was through the bench of bishops—or so it was perceived by his subjects—that the King was seeking to rule the country. As a result, when his policies proved unpalatable—as many of them did—it was the bishops who bore the brunt of the criticism. Opposition to the bishops provided an ideal rallying point for the diverse, often contradictory, social, political and religious interests which stood— seemingly united—behind the National Covenant. But in many respects, as was suggested above, that unity was much more apparent than real. It is time, therefore, that we looked more closely at what lay behind the alliance of ministers and magnates which spearheaded the covenanting movement and, more specifically, at the motives which prompted their animosity towards episcopacy.

As regards the ministers, it hardly needs saying that the committed presbyterians among them were by definition anti-episcopal. There was no place for bishops in the pure Melvillian scheme of church government. Still less was there room, given the presbyterians' belief in the complete separation of church and state, for the highly politicised episcopate created by Charles I. Doubtless to a man, the presbyterians would have echoed Wariston's sonorous condemnation of episcopacy as 'that great-grandmother of all our corruptions, novations, usurpations, diseases and troubles'.[6] Yet in 1638 presbyterians as committed as Wariston certainly was to 'the utter overthrow and ruin of episcopacy' were in a distinct minority. For the most part, the

Scottish clergy had conformed to the hybrid system of ecclesiastical government established by James VI. While James had ensured the reimposition of episcopacy, he had not sought to abolish the lower church courts—the kirk sessions and presbyteries—but had merely given the bishops a controlling interest in their operation. However grudgingly, the majority of ministers accepted this arrangement and it gradually became apparent to all but a few die-hards that bishop and presbytery could co-exist and even work in harmony. By the 1630s, just as there were few survivors—David Calderwood aside—who could recall first hand the epic battles between James VI and the Melvillians, so there were few new recruits prepared to follow in the footsteps of their embattled predecessors. The river of pure Melvillianism had been reduced to a trickle.

But it had not completely dried up. There did remain in Scotland a small but significant body of able, intelligent and energetic ministers whose commitment to presbyterianism remained unshaken by the success of James VI's experiment and was only reinforced by Charles I's promotion of Canterburian episcopacy. It was these men—led in the first instance by Alexander Henderson and David Dickson, minister of Irvine—who were the real architects of the covenanting revolution. A militant but well-organised minority, they were able in the later 1630s to exploit the growing discontent with Charles I's government and to radicalise the opposition as it developed, pushing the moderate clerical majority to ever more extreme solutions. They were in the short term astonishingly successful.

To be successful, however, this militant minority had to find some purchase among their less radical colleagues. In this respect, Charles I played straight into their hands, providing leverage in abundance, not just through his attitude to the bishops—though that was clearly not unimportant—but also through his attempts to alter the liturgy—the established rituals of public worship—in the reformed kirk. Such liturgical changes had in fact first been mooted by James VI who, in the interests of uniformity of worship throughout his British realms, had sought to bring Scottish practice into line with that of England. In 1618, for example, through the Five Articles of Perth, he had attempted to introduce kneeling at Holy Communion, the observance of Holy Days, private baptism and communion, and confirmation. Immensely proud of their own well-established forms of worship and deeply suspicious of the anglicising policies of the King, the Scots were appalled by these attempts to corrupt what they saw as the pristine purity of the kirk. Nevertheless, the King was able to force his proposals through a well-managed General Assembly at Perth in 1618 and, with greater difficulty, through a rather less well-managed parliament in 1621. But the extent of the opposition to the Five Articles warned him off trying to enforce them with any rigour and they were widely disregarded. King James apparently learned his lesson and did not pursue further his ultimate aim of rewriting the Scottish liturgy in conformity with that of England. But his son failed to take note of—or chose to ignore—his father's experience. By the time of his ill-fated visit to Scotland in 1633 it was well known that he intended introducing extensive liturgical reforms based on the practice of the English Canterburians.

Despite the distinctly audible rumblings of discontent, Charles I pressed ahead with his policy. The outcome was the publication in January 1636 of a Code of Canons which not only incorporated the Five Articles of Perth, but also intimated that a revised liturgy was in preparation and was shortly to be published. The new Prayer Book—'Laud's Liturgy'—finally appeared the following year. Its actual contents are of much less significance than the fact that, long before it was published, it was widely rumoured in Scotland to be not so much Canterburian as overtly Catholic in both substance and inspiration. Such fears were fanned by the manner in which it was prepared and introduced. Drawn up with minimal consultation and approved by neither General Assembly nor parliament, the Prayer Book was imposed on Scotland by virtue of the royal prerogative alone. The King's arbitrary handling of a highly-charged issue had presented the militant presbyterian minority with a perfect opportunity to further their aims. They made the most of it. The Edinburgh riots which greeted the first use of the Prayer Book in July 1637— what Wariston dubbed with heavy irony 'the fair, plausible and peaceable welcome the service book received in Scotland'[7]—were hardly spontaneous. On the contrary, they were large scale demonstrations orchestrated by men— Henderson and Dickson to the fore—who were not afraid to manipulate and exploit the prejudices of the mob.

The nature of these prejudices is nowhere better illustrated than in the writings of another young presbyterian zealot, Samuel Rutherford. In 1636, Rutherford was exiled from his parish of Anwoth in Kirkcudbrightshire for his persistent radicalism and packed off to Aberdeen in the fond but futile hope that contact with the conservative divines of the north-east would promote his theological re-education. Unable to preach and bereft of genuine companionship, the intensely pious Rutherford maintained a wide-ranging correspondence in which he poured out—often in vividly sensual detail— the unrequited yearnings of his tortured soul for spiritual transcendence. Yet for all his mystical piety—virtually unique in the annals of Scottish presbyterianism—Rutherford could also be both extremely practical and bitterly partisan. Among his correspondents, significantly enough, were not only Henderson and Dickson, but also prominent lay covenanters such as Lords Balmerino and Loudoun. If this is additional testimony to the close-knit nature of the group which was to oversee the revolution, the letters— particularly those to his own former parishioners—also indicate the nature of the popular prejudices which they sought to exploit. For example, writing to Anwoth just ten days before the Prayer Book was introduced, Rutherford warned his flock in no uncertain terms of the terrible fate at God's hands which awaited those who 'turned from the good old way to the dog's vomit again'. That the 'dog's vomit' consisted, among other things, of the Five Articles, the Canons and the Prayer Book is evident from what follows:

> I counsel you to beware of the new and strange leaven of men's inventions, beside and against the word of God, contrary to the oath of the kirk, now coming among you. I instructed you of the superstition and idolatry in kneeling in the instant of the Lord's Supper, and of crossing in baptism, and of men's

days without any warrant of Christ our perfect Lawgiver. Countenance not the surplice, the attire of the mass-priest, the garment of Baal's priest. The abominable bowing to altars of wood is coming upon you: Hate and keep yourselves from idols. Forbear in any case to hear the reading of the new service book, full of gross heresies, popish and superstitious errors, without any warrant of Christ, tending to the overthrow of preaching. You owe no obedience to the bastard canons; they are unlawful, blasphemous and superstitious. All the ceremonies that lie in Antichrist's foul womb, the wares of that great mother of fornications, the kirk of Rome, are to be refused.[8]

Rutherford was nothing if not colourful in his letter writing. But rhetoric of this kind echoed up and down the land on the eve of the revolution. Drawing on a long-standing, now almost pathological fear of Roman Catholicism and reflecting on the allegedly singular purity of the reformed Scottish kirk, it proved powerfully effective as a means of mobilising popular opposition to the King's religious innovations.

At the same time, moreover, it could be used to blacken still further the name of episcopacy. For indeed the bishops, albeit reluctantly led by Spottiswoode, had helped to draw up the new liturgy and did comply, whatever their misgivings, with the King's instructions for its introduction in July 1637. As a result the presbyterians were not only able to portray the Prayer Book as crypto-Catholic at best, but also to find the bishops guilty by association of pro-papal leanings. In the eyes of the zealots, the bishops were quite simply agents of the antichristian church of Rome who, having no warrant in Scripture, had no place in a truly reformed kirk. Ultimately, or so the radicals believed, the bishops had not simply to be removed, but their office had to be formally and finally abjured. It was, however, some time before they dared openly canvas the abjuration of episcopacy in this way. The radicals were well aware that many of their more moderate clerical colleagues, while sharing their suspicions about the Romanising tendencies of the Canterburians, were less than convinced that the episcopal office itself had no Scriptural warrant. There were many, like Robert Baillie, who hankered after the good old days of James VI and who would have settled simply for 'limitations' or 'cautions' being placed on the nature and extent of the bishops' powers. In consequence, the radicals were obliged to proceed more cautiously, more subtly and with more regard to ecclesiastical and constitutional precedent than their violent invective might at first lead one to suspect.

The most telling example of this is of course the National Covenant itself. Drafted by Henderson and Wariston towards the end of February 1638, the most noteworthy feature of the National Covenant—aside from its dullness— is its conservatism. Essentially a list of statutes favourable to the reformed kirk, it ventures no overt criticism of the King and no overt mention of episcopacy. It was a document made deliberately vague so as to appeal to a spectrum of opinion which was as diverse and contradictory as it was wide. Yet at the same time the very form of the covenant appealed to ideas of spiritual renewal and national regeneration which were deeply embedded in the Scottish Protestant tradition. It should come as no surprise to find Wariston talking in terms of the 'glorious marriage day of the kingdom with God'.[9] Scotland was a covenanted nation and the renewal of the covenant created a mood of great urgency and still greater expectancy. As Rutherford never tired of repeating, little Scotland was the bride of Christ and, as such, was engaged in a struggle with Antichrist which was cosmic in its dimensions as well as apocalyptic in its implications. Scotland, for him, was playing a leading role in events which presaged the latter days of the world.

In the fevered atmosphere created by such expectations, exacerbated still further by the virtual collapse of the crown's authority, the National Covenant proved a remarkably effective focus of opposition. First signed in Greyfriars' Churchyard in Edinburgh on 28 February, copies were rapidly circulated around the country and attracted near unanimous support in almost every corner of the realm except the north-east. In so far as they thought at all about the content as opposed to the form of the covenant, the majority of signatories evidently believed that they were protesting merely against the unconstitutional manner in which the Canons and the Prayer Book had been introduced. As was later revealed, however, its authors believed that the National Covenant contained proof positive that episcopacy too was unlawful. For incorporated within the National Covenant was the Negative Confession of 1581, a document consisting largely of a detailed abjuration of those many aspects of popery which were thought abhorrent and detestable—including, crucially, the papacy's 'wordly monarchy and wicked hierarchy'. Apparently unbeknown to many of the National Covenant's signatories, this was a phrase which the presbyterians had no hesitation in construing as a reference to and condemnation of episcopacy. In effect, if such an interpretation were deemed correct, a great many Scots—not least the moderate clergy—had been duped into signing a document with which they did not necessarily or whole-heartedly agree. Whether or not one attributes this masterly piece of decep-tion to Wariston's forensic skills, there is no doubt that written into the fine print of the National Covenant was a crucial clause which the radicals could—and did—invoke to their considerable advantage.

But as yet it was still not clear to the militants that clerical opinion could be so manipulated—or so intimidated—as to ensure the removal of epis-copacy root and branch. At this stage, in the early months of 1638, it was more politic to focus public attention on the outrage which the imposition of the Prayer Book and the Canons was generally seen to represent. Yet in private the presbyterians were already uncovering a quite gratifying level of support for their attitude to episcopacy. This emanated, however, not so much from the clergy as from the laity. Among laymen, and especially among the nobility, resentment at the political heights to which the bishops had been elevated ran deep. One leading lay covenanter, John Leslie, sixth Earl of Rothes, began his personal memoir of the events of 1637-38 with a sweeping attack on the bishops whom he believed—'having encroached so by degrees'—were responsible for loosing a 'flood of illegal violence to overflow the truth of religion and liberties of the subject'.[10] Rothes, together with two other prominent noblemen, James Elphinstone, Lord Balmerino, and John Campbell, Lord Loudoun, sat on the small committee which revised and finally approved Wariston's draft of the National Covenant. All three had a history of opposition to Charles I's regime; all three had suffered real or imagined slights at the hands of the episcopate; and all three were intent—at the very least—on stripping the bishops of the secular powers which they had recently acquired. It is not hard to imagine such men being more than susceptible to the arguments of Wariston for the wholesale extirpation of the episcopal bench. But the same in fact applies to the nobility as a whole for, whether or not they were committed presbyterians, the landed elite had sound political reasons for being hostile to Charles I's government in general and his bishops in particular.

The Scottish aristocracy had a great deal to grumble about in the late 1630s. For over a century, rising prices and falling rent-rolls had been eroding their incomes and, in the view of some historians, threatening the very fabric of the economic order on which were founded both their social status and their political power. If this is so—and the argument perhaps deserves more credit than it is sometimes accorded—the policies of Charles I served only to deepen an existing crisis. His celebrated Act of Revocation, for example, hurriedly issued in the first year of his reign, was viewed by many noblemen as a quite unprecedented and wholly unconstitutional assault on their landed wealth, their jurisdictional rights over their tenants and hence on their traditional authority in the localities. The details of the Revocation need not concern us here, but it is significant that, from the very outset of his reign, the King found himself at loggerheads with the Scottish ruling elite. The nobility, already made uneasy by their fluctuating economic fortunes, were made to feel decidedly uncomfortable by royal policies which appeared to undermine the basis of their privileged and hitherto unchallenged position in local society. Thus aroused, the climate of suspicion was never fully dispelled.

To make matters worse, it was not just in the localities that the nobility felt threatened, but also at the centre of power. The problem here stemmed originally from the Union of the Crowns of 1603 and the removal of the royal court to London. The union dramatically altered the traditionally close and informal relationship between the Scottish crown and the Scottish aristocracy, distancing the latter from the decision making processes and depriving them of an effective political voice. While James VI was on the throne, the full significance of this was to some extent obscured by his vast experience of Scottish problems and his long familiarity with most of the leading Scottish politicians. Charles I, born in Dunfermline but long since thoroughly anglicised, could boast neither of these advantages. Nor, characteristically, when he came to the throne did he make any attempt to compensate for the lack of them by continuing to rely on the privy councillors who had for twenty years mediated with such skill between James VI and his Scottish subjects. On the contrary, Charles at once set about dismantling the conciliar system which had served his father so well, ridding himself of councillors who were likely to prove obstructive and replacing them by political nonentities whose major—or sole—qualification for office was a willingness to do the King's bidding. The consensual approach to Scottish government, founded on the mediating role of a privy council trusted by both King and aristocracy, was swiftly jeopardised. At the same time, the extent to which the union had diminished the nobility's influence over the crown—rendering them, in effect, politically impotent—was exposed as never before.

This was brought sharply home to the Scots in 1633 when Charles I paid his promised, but long-postponed visit to Scotland for his coronation. The whole affair was a disaster and a ruinously expensive one into the bargain. Not only had the King taken an insultingly long time to embark on his pilgrimage north, but his stay was insultingly short—little more than a month—and he was clearly delighted to see the back of his native realm at the earliest opportunity. More significantly, in political terms the visit made plain what little store Charles set by the advice of—or even consultation with—the Scottish landed elite. For some years, between 1628 and 1633, Charles had been protected from the folly of his own ignorance and the fury of the Scottish aristocracy by placing some reliance on the advice of William Graham, Earl of Menteith. Mentieth was both sufficiently sensitive to Scottish issues and sufficiently trusted by the King to mitigate the full effects of royal policy in Scotland. But in 1633, on the eve of the King's visit, Menteith fell from power and there was no one to take his place as an unofficial adviser on Scottish matters or to prevent the King riding roughshod over the interests and prejudices of his Scottish subjects. The consequences hardly augured well for the future. When, for example, parliament met briefly to consider, among other things, certain religious innovations, the King did his utmost to gag discussion and ostentatiously sat and took note of those with the temerity to vote against his proposals. Moreover, when the discontented tried to approach the King by way of a written supplication, he not only refused to receive their petition, but had Balmerino arrested, tried and convicted of treason for being in possession of a copy of it.

Although Balmerino was subsequently pardoned, actions such as these were hardly calculated to endear Charles I to the Scottish nobility. Indeed, in political terms, it was sheer lunacy. Even as staunch a royalist as the poet William Drummond of Hawthornden was galvanised into action by the King's outrageous treatment of Balmerino. Drummond had no sympathy with Balmerino's presbyterian views, but on the eve of his trial in July 1635, the poet composed an *Apologetical Letter* in which he upheld Balmerino's right to petition the monarch and subjected the King's government to some trenchant criticism. He even went so far as to furnish Charles I with the quite astonishing piece of advice that he should read George Buchanan's *De jure regni apud Scotos* 'for his own private and the public good'.[11] To find Wariston perusing the radical political tracts of Buchanan and other advocates of tyrannicide occasions very little surprise. To find the loyal and conservative Drummond actually recommending them to the King is both a telling indictment of Charles I's government of Scotland and eloquent testimony to the mounting anxiety of the landed elite.

Of course Drummond's real point was by no means radical. He was concerned simply, as he put it, that 'the voice of the people should not be kept from the ears of a prince'. He therefore went on to implore the King to listen to those—primarily the nobility—who in all sincerity were interested in 'amending disorders and bettering the form of his government'.[12] In this respect, the poet was in fact doing no more than to articulate the deep-rooted prejudices of the landed elite as a whole. It was a commonplace of contemporary political thought that the nobility were duty-bound by birth and breeding to advise the monarch, while the monarch was in turn obliged to seek out that advice and to consult with his born counsellors, the leading men of the kingdom. Where Drummond betrayed his essential conservatism was in his belief that such consultation—however highly to be commended— was nevertheless undertaken entirely at the discretion of what he described as a 'loving prince'. The King, insisted Drummond, was not accountable to the nobility for any of his actions and the nobility had no right—under any circumstances—to disobey or to resist his will. Charles I was accountable to God and to God alone.

What lay behind this heavy emphasis on the duty of unstinting obedience to the crown was an acute fear that political dissent would culminate in civil war and civil war in social anarchy. In another pamphlet, written in the fateful year of 1638 and aptly entitled *Irene*, Drummond reiterated his belief that absolute obedience was fundamental to the preservation of political order and argued that the resistance then clearly being contemplated by the covenanting leadership could only lead to the dissolution of the state and the disintegration of society.[13] Such fears as these—ultimately, after all, to be vindicated—were undoubtedly shared by many among the landed elite. In all probability they also preyed uneasily on the consciences of the covenanting leadership. Certainly these men were not social or political revolutionaries, far less—as their opponents sometimes charged—republicans. It was no part of their intention to overthrow monarchical government. They were intent rather on restoring it to the form in which—in their own estimation—it had functioned in the past. If anyone was a revolutionary, it was a monarch who, in ignoring the advice of his born counsellors, was flouting age-old conventions and traditions of government. The covenanting nobility were seeking only to recreate an ideal political order in which crown and aris-tocracy *together* governed the realm.

Yet the problem remained unresolved as to how this was to be achieved without defying the authority of their anointed but stubbornly unco-operative sovereign, Charles I. So long as the King refused to recognise or participate in the aristocracy's idealising nostalgia for a past political order, treasonable resistance appeared the only alternative to meek acquiescence in the face of an arbitrary royal will. At this point, however, the bishops emerged— conveniently enough—from the shadows to rescue the landed elite from the awful consequences of confronting their conservative consciences head-on. For could it not be argued that the King himself bore no responsibility for the ill-judged policies being pursued in Scotland? Was it not rather his evil and upstart counsellors—the bishops—who were to blame? Not only then was Charles innocent, but the nobility could not themselves be accused of dis-obeying and resisting him. On the contrary, they were defying the bishops for the sake of the King. What appeared to be acts of resistance to Charles I were in reality displays of loyalty to him. Such a scenario will be instantly recognisable to anyone familiar with the rebellions of the medieval aristocracy in Scotland and elsewhere. The cry of evil counsel and the lynching of allegedly evil counsellors was a common enough way of protesting against royal policy without incurring a charge of treason through challenging directly the sovereign himself. It was a fiction not only of surpassing convenience, but one which had seriously distorted the Scottish nobility's reading of their own feudal past.

The point is well illustrated in the principal historical work—the *Annales of Scotland*—of Sir James Balfour of Denmilne. Balfour was a distinguished antiquary with an interest in history in general and heraldry in particular who rose in the 1630s to a position of some prominence as Lord Lyon King of Arms, the senior heraldic office in Scotland. In this capacity he officiated at the coronation of Charles I in 1633. Subsequently, however, he became disillusioned with the administration he was appointed to serve and spent much of his time in semi-retirement compiling an invaluable work chronicling Scotland's history from the reign of Malcolm Canmore in the eleventh century down to that of Charles I in his own day. While the *Annales* are primarily a monument to seventeenth-century antiquarian scholarship, they also bear witness to the nostalgic conservatism of a landed gentleman who firmly believed that in the past the key to the good governance of the realm had lain in the traditionally close relationship between the crown and the aristocracy. But in the present, in the dark days of the 1630s, this relationship—and with it the welfare of the kingdom—was under threat, not so much from the Union of the Crowns nor even from the defects of the King himself, but from the evil machinations of the ambitious, upstart counsellors—'these unhappy bishops'—who had come to dominate Charles I's privy council.[14]

In the perspective of history, Balfour had little difficulty in finding the bishops responsible for the myriad problems which afflicted Scotland in the 1630s. 'They were evil counsellors', he wrote, 'but worse musicians: for they tempered their strings to such a pitch of ambition and superstitious foolery, that before ever they yielded any sound, they burst all in pieces'.[15] As far as Balfour was concerned, the bishops were the precise contemporary equivalent of the self-seeking upstarts—the 'mushrooms' as he liked to call them—who had troubled Scottish monarchs in the past. With more relish than accuracy, for example, he described how in 1482 the Scottish nobility had saved King James III from the corrupting influence of his low-born favourites by having them summarily hanged at Lauder Bridge. The King, opined Balfour, 'had addicted himself totally to the counsel of Thomas Cochrane, William Rodger and James Hommill, mushrooms sprung up out of the dregs of the commons, whom he had raised to overtop his nobility, misgovern the country, and foster him in his lusts, riots and wicked courses'. James III was well rid of such sycophantic parasites. A much more appealing model of kingship was provided by his son and successor, James IV, who, according to Balfour's approving analysis, made 'choice of a select number of the nobility and gentry to be of his privy council and did solemnly promise to do nothing in the government without their counsel and advice'.[16] Here in a nutshell was the landed elite's ideal version of their feudal past and it was one with clear implications for the role of bishops in Charles I's government. In Balfour's view, the bishops were simply upstarts—mushrooms—intent on advancing themselves 'to overrule both church and state contrary to the laws of God and this nation'. They had usurped the functions of the nobility, monopolised the ear of the King, and were imposing policies on Scotland which were bound to alienate the people from their prince. It was the bishops who were to blame for the debacle of the 1633 parliament; the bishops who had engineered the trial of the innocent Balmerino; the bishops who were responsible for the Canons and the Prayer Book; and the bishops who were driving covenanted Scots—reluctantly—into armed rebellion.[17]

Admittedly this is merely the testimony of one man. Yet as Scotland's senior herald Balfour perhaps does have some claim to speak for the landed, arms-bearing, elite. In any case, it seems not unreasonable to suggest that Balfour's vision of Scotland's past—not least his understanding of the traditional relationship between the crown and the aristocracy—was widely shared by the embattled political community of the later 1630s. Likewise, it seems not unreasonable to suggest that, in the same way as Balfour, the lay leaders of Scottish society found it both convenient and consoling to sidestep a direct confrontation with Charles I by heaping their grievances on the heads of his unfortunate bishops. The bishops were an ideal scapegoat for both the inadequacies of the King's government and—just as important—the inhibitions of their own conservative consciences. Thus the basis of the unlikely alliance between the radical presbyterians and the conservative nobility becomes more understandable. They were indeed, though for very different reasons, at one in their detestation of episcopacy. At the same time, moreover, in the light of this, the Glasgow Assembly emerges as an occasion of critical significance. For not only did it witness the final abjuration of episcopacy, but thereby it also—paradoxically enough—exposed the underlying brittleness of the covenanting coalition.

At this point it is time, by way of conclusion, to return to the Glasgow Assembly itself. It was suggested earlier that the elections to the Assembly were deliberately rigged by the covenanting leadership. What lay behind this blatant gerrymandering was the imperative need to engineer the attendance with voting rights of sufficient laymen to ensure that, together with the rump of committed presbyterian clerics, they could successfully challenge and overthrow the authority of the bishops. By the late summer of 1638 it was no longer possible to fudge the strongly anti-episcopal interpretation which the militant presbyterians had from the outset placed on the Negative Confession and hence on the National Covenant. Yet it was still by no means clear that their more moderate colleagues could be persuaded to go beyond placing 'cautions' or 'limitations' on the exercise of episcopal power. The covenanting leadership was thus faced with the prospect of an Assembly dominated by a clerical majority with deep misgivings about their 'hidden' agenda of abolishing and abjuring episcopacy. The moderates had therefore to be outvoted and/or intimidated and the best way to achieve this was to pack the Assembly with sympathetic laymen of substantial social importance. This was accomplished partly by resurrecting and re-interpreting the role of 'ruling elders' in the hierarchy of ecclesiastical courts established under the presbyterian system. The mechanics of the elections and the manner in which they were manipulated are of bewildering complexity and need not detain us here. What is important is that the covenanting leadership was able to ensure that powerful local landowners were elected to sit alongside the ministers as representatives—commissioners—of each of Scotland's sixty-three presbyteries. This may not have produced the desired numerical majority, but the election of 17 peers, 9 knights and 25 lairds—not to mention 47 burgh commissioners—did ensure a substantial lay presence whose influence was far out of proportion to its numbers. In addition, and here the covenanters fell back on blatant intimidation, they instructed that any nobleman who had signed the National Covenant might attend the Assembly; that 4-6 gentlemen from each presbytery were to accompany their commissioners as what they euphemistically termed 'assessors'; that each burgh commissioner was also to be attended by up to 6 lay assessors; and that—just to make sure that no sympathetic layman of substance need feel excluded—gentlemen not chosen as commissioners or assessors might attend in any case of their own volition. This was surely loading the dice with a vengeance. While none of these latter groups had voting rights, their very presence in such numbers would prove sufficient to overawe all but the most independently-minded of the moderate clergy.

Small wonder, then, that Glasgow Cathedral was thronged to bursting point in November 1638; small wonder too that the bishops themselves did not dare to attend the Assembly; and small wonder that their supporters among the moderate clergy—with the sole exception of the querulous but conscientious Baillie—were terrorised into complete acquiescence in the dissolution of the episcopal order. In fact, the proceedings of the Assembly went better than even the most optimistic of the covenanting leadership could have hoped. The King's Commissioner, the Marquis of Hamilton, never really stood a chance of controlling it. He was outmanoeuvred at virtually every turn by the astuteness of Henderson, the resourcefulness of Wariston and, perhaps above all, by the fact that both he and his opponents knew well enough that whatever concessions he made in the King's name, Charles I would never stand by them. On 28 November, a week after the proceedings had begun, Hamilton abandoned the Assembly to its own devices, the dignity of his retreat marred only by the fact that the door of the Cathedral was locked and the key temporarily mislaid. Under the circumstances, one feels a certain sympathy for the Commissioner when he complained piteously to the King that 'next Hell I hate this place'.[18]

With Hamilton gone, the Assembly got down to the real business in hand. The commissioners worked extremely hard: as Baillie put it with evident satisfaction, it was resolved 'to have but one session in the day, to sit from 10 or 11 [in the morning], to 4 or 5 [in the evening], so we were all relieved of the expense of a dinner'.[19] After much debate—enriched, no doubt, by hunger—the Assembly passed a long and historic series of measures which rejected the liturgical reforms recently introduced by the King, overturned the established ecclesiastical system and, in so doing, created a constitutional crisis which would be resolved only by recourse to arms. On 6 December, the Canons and the Prayer Book were annulled; on 8 December, episcopacy was abjured and removed; on 10 December, the Five Articles were condemned; on 13 December, the bishops were individually deposed and excommunicated; on 19 December, clerics were forbidden to hold civil office; and on 20 December, annual General Assemblies were reinstituted. Within two weeks, the Glasgow Assembly had done its work. The covenanting revolution was well underway.

Yet as the commissioners dispersed and the euphoria over their triumphantly successful handling of the Assembly died down, the leaders of the covenanting movement may well have paused to consider some more sobering reflections. The seemingly united front presented by the Assembly was after all the product of terror tactics rather than a spontaneously achieved consensus. Moreover, and perhaps more seriously still, in destroying the episcopate, the Assembly had also destroyed the basis of the alliance between the ministers and magnates. With the bishops gone, the landed elite could no longer indulge in the luxury of using them as scapegoats for the evils of the King's government. Many, perhaps most, will have known all along that the 'evil counsellors argument' was no more than a smokescreen, a device which shielded them from having to confront directly either the King or their own consciences. In the course of the Assembly, however, the smoke gave way to fire and illuminated for all to see the true nature of the problem. And the problem was of course King Charles I himself. A King whose commitment to his religion was as profound as that of any presbyterian, but a King whose comprehension of the art of politics was as non-existent as his understanding of his Scottish subjects. Temperamentally incapable of compromise and conciliation, Charles I viewed political grievances as personal insults and a king's promises as ever frangible. His attitude is well conveyed by his justly infamous instructions to Hamilton during the protracted negotiations preceding the Glasgow Assembly: 'flatter them with what hopes you please', he told his Commissioner, 'until I be ready to suppress them'.[20]

Yet despite this the Scottish landed elite clung hopelessly to the belief that Charles I would one day fulfil their antiquated expectations of kingship and govern Scotland in the way they imagined it had been governed in the past. They opposed him, defied him, went to war with him, but all the time protesting their fundamental loyalty to him. Like Drummond of Hawthornden, the rebel nobility knew only too well that they, the King and the social and political order they collectively represented must ultimately stand or fall together. Gradually, however, in the years after 1638, they lost control of those radical elements in the covenanting movement whose ideas were fundamentally at variance with their own. The presbyterian radicals wanted to reshape society in their image of godliness. The conservative nobility wanted to recreate it in their image of an idealised feudal past. The two aims were essentially contradictory. Moreover, unfortunately for the nobility, so long as Charles I refused to lend substance to their idealising nostalgia, the cycle of violence and revolution escalated and the presbyterians grew ever more powerful. But perhaps Balfour may be permitted the last word, for in a passage in his *Annales* written in the late 1640s, he captured quite succinctly not only the self-deluding loyalism of the landed elite, but also their mounting fear in the face of the overweening ambition of the presbyterian zealots:

> It is to be remembered, the chiefest bellows that has blown this terrible fire, were first the unhappy bishops of both kingdoms; and now the preachers and ministers ... who in lieu of obedience and conformity to government, and compliance with the necessities of so good and religious a King, did teach and obtrude to the people ... nothing more than Christ's cause, religion, liberty and privilege of the subject, whereby they have not only embittered the affection of the vassal but in effect quite poisoned them against their native sovereign and prince.[21]

NOTES

1. What follows is a modified version of a lecture first delivered to the Society of Friends of Glasgow Cathedral and subsequently published by them as *The Glasgow Assembly 1638* (Glasgow, 1988). I am grateful to the Society for permission to have it reprinted here.
2. *The Letters and Journals of Robert Baillie*, ed. David Laing (Bannatyne Club, 1841-42), vol. i, 118-76. Baillie's account of the Glasgow Assembly is given in a long letter to his cousin, William Spang, minister of the Scots kirk at Campvere, written up from notes some six months after the events he described. Quotations from Baillie and other contemporary sources are rendered in modern English.
3. *Ibid.*, vol. i, 121.
4. *The Diary of Sir Archibald Johnston of Wariston 1632-1639*, ed. G.M. Paul (Scottish History Society, 1911), 400-1.
5. Baillie, *Letters and Journals*, vol. i, 124.
6. Wariston, *Diary 1632-1639*, 347.
7. *Ibid.*, 265.
8. *The Letters of Samuel Rutherford*, ed. A.A. Bonar (Edinburgh and London, 1894), 440.
9. Wariston, *Diary 1632-1639*, 322.
10. John, Earl of Rothes, *A Relation ... of the Affairs of the Kirk of Scotland* (Bannatyne Club, 1830), 1ff.
11. *The Works of William Drummond of Hawthornden*, ed. Thomas Ruddiman and John Sage (Edinburgh, 1711), 134.
12. *Ibid.*, 133.
13. *Ibid.*, 163-73.
14. For the *Annales*, see *The Historical Works of Sir James Balfour*, ed. James Haig (Edinburgh, 1824-25), vols. i and ii, *passim*.
15. *Ibid.*, vol. ii, 140.
16. *Ibid.*, vol. i, 205-6, 217-18.
17. *Ibid.*, vol. ii, 262, 200, 216, 223ff.
18. Quoted in David Stevenson, *The Scottish Revolution 1637-1644: The Triumph of the Covenanters* (Newton Abbot, 1973), 122.
19. Baillie, *Letters and Journals*, vol. i, 128.
20. Quoted in Gordon Donaldson, *Scotland: James V—James VII* (Edinburgh, 1965), 317.
21. Balfour, *Historical Works*, vol. iii, 426.

Note on Further Reading

While the interpretation of events offered here is entirely my own responsibility, I am enormously indebted to the many historians who have dealt with the period at more length and in more detail than is possible within the confines of a single essay. The best introduction to the political and religious issues covered here is volume 3 of the Edinburgh History of Scotland: Gordon Donaldson, *Scotland: James V—James VII* (Edinburgh, 1965). Maurice Lee Jr., *The Road to Revolution: Scotland under Charles I 1625-1637* (Urbana and Chicago, 1985), is a lucid and very readable account of how relations between the King and his Scottish subjects deteriorated so rapidly, while David Stevenson, *The Scottish Revolution 1637-44: The Triumph of the Covenanters* (Newton Abbot, 1973), carries the story forward into the revolutionary era and contains an excellent chapter on the Glasgow Assembly itself. As its subtitle implies,

Walter Makey, *The Church of the Covenant 1637-51: Revolution and Social Change in Scotland* (Edinburgh, 1979), approaches the covenanting period from a social and economic perspective and provides many valuable insights into the changes in the nature of Scottish society which lay behind the events of 1638 and their aftermath. Of more specialist interest, Gordon Donaldson, *The Making of the Scottish Prayer Book of 1637* (Edinburgh, 1954), and David Mullan, *Episcopacy in Scotland: The History of an Idea 1560-1638* (Edinburgh, 1986), both repay detailed study.

N.B. Since this note was written a pamphlet has appeared by David Stevenson, *The Covenanters* (Saltire Society, 9 Fountain Close, Edinburgh) which gives a readable, authoritative general account of the background to the issues discussed in this and the next chapter.—T.B.

2 A BANNER WITH A STRANGE DEVICE: THE LATER COVENANTERS

V.G. Kiernan

Shadows of martyrdom hung over Scotland much later than England, when Bloody Mary's doings had receded into a forgettable past. Many families in the eighteenth century could look back to involvement on one side or the other in Scotland's Time of Troubles, or on both sides. A great-uncle of David Hume was hanged at Edinburgh in 1682 as a covenanter, 'after a particularly dubious trial'; his great-grandfather John, a loose-living army man, sat on the jury that sent the covenanting minister Renwick to the gallows in 1688.[1] As years wore on, Scotsmen of nearly all colours could join in respect for that band of stubborn sufferers of the years after 1660. Their memory came back more brightly to life during the early nineteenth century when national rights and struggles were making a great stir in the world, and Scotsmen felt conscious of something they had lost, a vacancy not to be filled with tartan trumpery alone. Scott could not restrain a Tory inclination to satirise the men of the moors, but he could not withhold some admiration as well. His more stridently conservative son-in-law Lockhart was at pains to defend *Old Mortality* from the charge of 'scoffing and irreverence'; it had quickly taken its place, he declared, in Scottish cottages, side by side with the Bible and the old rude chronicles of the seventeenth-century wars. He quoted Wordsworth's tributes to the covenanters in *The Excursion*.[2]

James Hogg was easily talked by his Edinburgh friends or patrons into subscribing to their Tory politics, but he was really a very decent fellow with a heart in the right place—in the Ettrick Forest where he reared his sheep among mountains that once sheltered groups of fugitive covenanters. His 1817 novel *The Brownie of Bodsbeck*[3] about some of these, men from the west in hiding after Bothwell Brig, is the story of a worthy sheep-farmer and his daughter, who take pity on them and secretly give them food, until he is arrested by Claverhouse and his soldiers and dragged off to Edinburgh for trial. Hogg took his incidents from tales told by his father, and still 'fresh in the memory of our peasants'. His fugitives—'grey-bearded ministers, lairds, weavers, and poor hinds, all sharing the same hard fate'—are held up as heroic figures, even if wildly imprudent, and in spite of their being of the Cameronian persuasion, believers in retaliation instead of non-violence. Hogg's portrait of Claverhouse as a monster of capricious cruelty was drawn from local tradition; his character was still held 'in at least as great detestation

25

as that of the arch-fiend himself. Members of all the prominent local families too were arrested at one time or another, Hogg says, for attending conventicles; among them some of the Scotts of Harden, forbears of the novelist.

John Galt had ancestors who suffered in the persecution. His *Ringan Gilhaize, or The Covenanters* (1823) is a family chronicle covering the great age of the Kirk from 1558 and the Reformation to 1688 and its re-vindication against James II. Much to its author's satisfaction, it was 'the only novel ever recommended from a Scottish pulpit'.[4] It more than made up, as Galt intended, for the shortcomings of *Old Mortality*, by going to the other extreme and making dauntless idealists of all loyal reformers and covenanters, from high to low, always in the act of opening their bibles or drawing their swords. But Ringan in prison, consoled by a heavenly vision, is a reminder of how their self-dramatising religion, fed on the volcanic imagery of the Old Testament, could alleviate the drab existence of an obscure peasantry, and lend them human dignity by giving them a place in their country's life and in service to a cause. All the narrative shows us men and women under heavy stress trying to comprehend random events as parts of a divine plan, much as men of old turned scattered stars into an Archer or a Crab.

In a later day Robert Louis Stevenson left his long story *Heathercat* unfinished, because it may be he shared some of Scott's contradictory feelings. His unlucky laird of Montroymont is being slowly but surely reduced to bankruptcy by the fines incurred by his irresponsibly pious helpmate, a 'mad, raging, presbyterian zealot of a wife'—a higher-class relative of Scott's fanatical Mause, the bane of her unlucky son. The story breaks off with a prayer-meeting in the hills, a preacher's voice wrestling with dismal rain. In 1866 Stevenson wrote an account of the 1666 rising, drawn to it a good deal no doubt because it ended in his favourite Pentland Hills. In his conclusion he lamented that it had become 'the fashion of the day to jeer and to mock, to execrate and to contemn, the noble band'. A pernicious anglicising process had been at work on upper-class Scotland; and Englishmen, as Lockhart complained, thought of the Scottish peasantry as 'universally imbued with the most savage and covenanting fanaticism'. A Scottish working class would take over the inspiring memory of the covenanters that the literate had discarded. It in turn would forget, and twenty years ago there was not much left but 'denigration and oblivion'.[5]

The period from the Kirk's beginnings to the twilight of its national importance after 1660 can be read as a continuous history, as it was by Galt, though it was also a very erratic history. In a country like old Scotland, with an exceptionally conglomerate structure—a mixture of feudal, pre-feudal, and proto-capitalist—only a bizarre theology could be expected to take shape, though it might be one built like Calvinism on an irrational but rigid logic. It is another mark of Scotland's contorted annals that those of its martyrs who were men of the common people were less often rebels against feudal oppression, as so many thousands in other countries were, than religious devotees.

The problem of how to decipher those strange enthusiasts has been stated by Willy Thompson. It is beyond us to know how they viewed the social order; we cannot but suppose, nevertheless, that somehow their religious outlook 'expressed their view of acceptable and necessary relations between themselves and authority, and between social classes'.[6] It is much the same as with diseases of bygone times, whose symptoms no one recorded accurately enough for historians to be able to diagnose them. We can do no better than to look at the covenanters in their religious and social setting. Sometimes we may venture to read between the lines of what they said or wrote. Scotland was a poor, not seldom a famishing country, and the continual resort to biblical imagery of sheep and pasture may have had undertones of physical as well as spiritual hunger. An old woman talking to the celebrated preacher Peden expressed her enjoyment of the Bible by saying that God 'hath casten me the keys of the pantrie door and bids me take my fill'.[7]

Scotland's feudal structure was highly complex, partly because in addition to regional variations the sixteenth century saw shifts in landholding, particularly with widespread feuing of land, or perpetual grants at low and fixed rents. A good part of these shifts were set in motion by the decay and dispossession of the old Church. A cultivator seldom owned the land he worked, and his work was often poorly rewarded. Crops were thin, rents might be disproportionately high, rising to a third of gross output, so that, as Smout says, 'the peasant enjoyed only a small margin of subsistence', and was liable besides to other payments in kind or in services. Farming methods often involved joint activity and use of plough animals, which ought to have promoted peasant solidarity but may have had an opposite effect. Co-operation was 'socially difficult to achieve', according to Smout, and was accompanied by much wrangling and bickering. Security of tenure may have been commoner than used to be supposed. Leases may have grown longer, and customary rights might be strong even in the absence of legal warrant. Evictions may therefore have been 'relatively rare'.[8] But tenants at will had no such rights. In general, the infrequency of peasant revolts may be explained by cultivators having long been, as they were coming to be in England by the first half of the seventeenth century, too deeply separated by their conditions of life to be able to combine, at least for any rational purpose.

It may not be surprising if some strata of the peasantry learned to hold fast to a dogmatic creed as a substitute for the inherited patch of soil that peasants in other countries clung to. Smallholdings, as well as small estates, were however more numerous than elsewhere in the south-western area where attachment to Kirk teaching came to be warmest. It was a pastoral region, much of it hills and moorland, where some of the fertile scraps must have been too trifling and scattered to be brought together in the hands of great landowners. They contributed to a spirit of independence and self-assertion that could bolster firmness in religion. Here was one example of Scotland's division into provinces each with a character of its own. They might have evolved better as a federal league like Switzerland's, instead of being artificially united under a somewhat make-believe monarchy.

To R.L. Stevenson it seemed that through all the southern uplands antiquity was 'still living and active' in his own day, in their Celtic names and in 'a scarce-mingled Celtic population'.[9] Galloway in the far south-west was the area, as its name shows, that remained Gaelic longest. Here the Highlands reached down far southward, further south along the Mull of Kintyre than Berwick. North of Loch Trool stands Merrick, the highest hill in southern Scotland. Galloway hills had a prominent place in the annals of Wallace and Bruce; it was at Loch Trool, in 1307, that Bruce opened the campaign which closed seven years later at Bannockburn. Memories of those days hung over the Scotland of the Kirk. 'Two national epics', Christopher Harvie has remarked, 'treated the War of Independence ... as a popular struggle for nationalism which was also libertarian'. Since then the south-west had lain off the main track of conflict with England, and hence could feel less in need of royal protection. For English invaders the highroad was the east coast route, with Edinburgh only fifty miles from the border; it was the Scots who, after Flodden, made do with the backdoor route by way of Carlisle, for the last time in 1745.

Where a king was seldom seen, and feudalism was still rampant, there was endemic turbulence until the late sixteenth century. Apart from the Highlands 'the restive part of Scotland', as Wallace Notestein called it in *The Scot in History*, 'was along the southwest border, with Galloway and the surrounding country as a continuous center of disaffection'. 'To a great extent the West of Scotland', David Mathew in his *Scotland under Charles I* observes, 'as far as the nobles and lairds were concerned, existed as a self-contained society'. Each region had need of a provincial capital. Aberdeen was one such, in the north-east; the south-west had Glasgow.

The south-west had an economic life of its own as well, though one that gave it various links with the outside. Not being always self-sufficient in grain, it marketed some of its pastoral products in Edinburgh or beyond. Galloway jutted out into the Irish Sea, and for its towns, mostly on or close to the water, there could be trading with Ireland, the Isle of Man, and the string of small ports southward along the Cumbrian coast. Nearly a quarter of Scotland's fifty or so royal burghs lay in the south-west. Some were insignificant, yet in the war-tax assessments in 1645 Wigtown was rated as high as Lanark; and in the valuation rolls of the Scottish shires in July 1653, where Fife and Perthshire stood far the highest, Ayrshire came fourth, and both Dumfriesshire and Galloway (Wigtownshire with Kirkcudbrightshire) were above the poorest batch.[10]

An important clue to the contrast between west and east, and the changes going on under the surface of Scottish life, with their political and ideological consequences, must be the long-drawn inflation so well analysed by Makey. On his showing, the mid seventeenth century troubles were only 'the final episode of a social revolution' long preparing, under the pressure of a price-rise steeper than anywhere else in Europe. This could mean 'catastrophic' reduction of the real incomes of all whose receipts were fixed, like those of the Crown, and feu-payments, and money rents if these could not be enhanced. In eastern Scotland, where rents were usually paid in kind, there was an automatic adjustment; in the west they were often calculated in cash, of diminishing value. 'Inflation was nibbling at the foundations of the customary society', though in a piecemeal, spasmodic fashion. Meanwhile the feuing of church lands brought 'a vast transfer of wealth from superior to vassal', and increased importance for the heritor, the proprietor drawing the rents of any land, whatever his legal status, often a commercial rather than a feudal proprietor. Customary rents, especially in the west, might have become 'ludicrously low' by the time that hard-up landlords set about raising them and the transfer of wealth was 'abruptly halted and indeed violently reversed'. All the strivings and discords of the Kirk, throughout its first century, must be seen as an intrinsic part of a long era of crisis and change.[11]

All vocation and mission had deserted the old Church; the Kirk supplied fresh energy and purpose. But if the Wars of Independence may be called, as regards the liberation of the people, Scotland's first false dawn, the Reformation was the second. Each ended with the feudalists firmly in the saddle. As in all countries more or less, the Reformation in Scotland suffered from deep flaws; they were to lead it into the blind tracks that ended on the Galloway moors. It came prematurely, thrust on a country where it had few genuine adherents by political confusion and the conflicting pressures of two powerful neighbours. It was not led, as elsewhere, by an energetic monarchy: it began in insurrection, and while this left a long-smouldering spark of courage to defy the world, it left also an obsession with strict uniformity, as the prerequisite of unity of action.

A *Calvinist* reformation was a further anomaly, leaving Scotland the odd man out (with the partial exception of Holland) in Protestant Europe, especially north-west Europe where Ireland was the Catholic oddity. It resulted from the connection with France, where in 1559 a first general synod of 79 Huguenot congregations took place; and, even more, from there being no monarchy able and willing to head a Lutheran reformation, as in Scandinavia and much of Germany, or set up an Anglican-style Church. The alternative was a presbyterian system, through which lay interests could direct things in a more decentralised manner. Presbyterianism represented a federation of districts and provinces, well suited to Scotland, with a General Assembly at the summit. At each level laymen of the propertied classes might take part, and see fair play to themselves.

In Ayrshire in September 1562, a year before Mary Queen of Scots made a progress through the county, 78 nobles and lairds met to sign a covenant to uphold the gospel. Glasgow University, the south-west's intellectual centre, was developing contacts with French strongholds of Protestant thinking. In such a region, with a rough social integration of its own in a blend of feudal and clan patriarchy, presbyterianism could seem natural enough, and in course of time some of the landowners could become genuinely attached to it. It could stand for neighbourliness and fraternity, in spite of social injustices which were scarcely felt as such because no other kind of life had yet dawned on men's minds. Old feudal centrifugalism could continue, adopting a new pattern in the form of championship of Kirk claims to freedom from government dictation. In all classes Calvinist intransigence would be sharpened by the proximity of Catholic Ireland.

It was only slowly and spasmodically that a regular presbyterian structure covering the whole country could be built up, while episcopacy faded into the background. An Act of the General Assembly in 1592 attempted to regulate its workings, with the apparent intention of ensuring a majority of ministers in the Assembly while leaving it possible for laymen to dominate the elections to it.[12] Laymen of the more serious kind were very much like Puritans in England, whose ideal, as Collinson shows, was a combination of clergy and magistrature in an endeavour to cement a social order crumbling at its edges by imposing a godly discipline on both high and low.[13] This partnership could work most effectively in a burgher setting like Edinburgh, where Kirk elders were regularly drawn from the civic oligarchy. To conservatives such as most ministers came to be, 'deference to social superiors', as Stevenson says, 'seemed natural and right'; they thought it equally natural for their inferiors to look up to *them*. Too much of the Kirk's teaching hardened into arid negatives, like the ban on dancing; while its repudiation of the arts threw an excessive weight on the intellectual aspects of religion, a theology in whose knots and coils a great many minds tied themselves up.

In the early days of the Reformation the struggling Kirk was sometimes ready to talk of social justice, and among some ministers of a more idealistic turn, and some ordinary folk especially in out of the way places, memories of this must have lingered. For them the Kirk could embody aspirations to a happier as well as more virtuous life here below. Radical ideas could be rekindled later on when the times were out of joint, as they usually were in Scotland, though with more emphasis on the Kirk's independence than on its obligations to the poor, and with a channelling off of social discontent as the outcome, instead of remedies for it. In the 1590s, a decade of dearth and disturbances, Andrew Melville was calling for fuller freedom of action for the Kirk, with elders of a new sort. In the original Reforming congregations elders had been freely elected; it was Scotland's first taste of democracy. But to repeat it on a national scale would have been a hazardous proposal. Melville wanted elders to be incorporated into the Kirk as salaried assistants, with partly spiritual functions.

In his later years, away in London, James VI succeeded in superimposing bishops on the Kirk, and though its presbyterian system was otherwise left untouched its parliament, the Assembly, was never allowed to meet between 1616 and 1638. This paralysis of the Kirk at its summit must help to explain the poor leadership of the 1638-60 era; also the lack of unity, because the long sleep of the Assembly left regional tendencies like those of the southwest and the north-east to mature more freely, and to incubate hostile factions. Charles I put a heavier strain on the *modus vivendi* by employing his bishops too much in matters of government, as part of the centralising programme adopted in one degree or another by all the European monarchies of the time. For the Kirk to be made more useful, it had to be made more respectable, by being better paid, instead of left to suffer from the inflation. Stipends were augmented by both James and Charles; Edinburgh ministers were on their way to being 'enormously richer', says Walter Makey, than the humble majority of their listeners. This improvement would satisfy many; but extension of royal authority must mean further encroachments on the Kirk's treasured autonomy.

In 1637 the prayerbook issue stirred a public excitement that all who felt threatened by Charles's policies could take advantage of. They included the nobility, whose alliance the Kirk needed just as Knox had done long before. In each case it would turn into a suffocating bear's hug; but it was not easy to calculate in advance whether Kirk freedom had more to fear from Whitehall and its prelates than from feudalists with a foot inside the Kirk's door. Aristocratic opposition, Makey suggests, came most firmly from Fife and the west. An appeal to religion, which was at the same time an appeal to Scottish patriotism, was the only way for the nobility to enlist public support. Its other hold on Scottish affections, here and there, was clan loyalty, but this was too divisive to contribute to a national movement. The Covenant signed so enthusiastically in 1638 was a stepping-stone from old feudal and clan feeling towards a new national consciousness; at the same time it was, like all nationalism, a barrier against the emergence of *class* consciousness. In this light it would be welcome to any in the propertied classes who saw reason to fear mass discontent. One cause of this might be that taxation had been stiffening in recent years, and now bore on a larger number of people.[14]

Indistinct and contradictory enough, the Covenant was a pledge that Scots would stand together in defence of 'the true reformed religion'. Its title had often been loosely affixed to much smaller matters. At Boston in 1615 John Cotton and his fellow-Puritans 'entered into a covenant with the Lord', and there were gibes at a ' "pretended covenant" ' binding the members of another group to watch and admonish one another.[15] Somehow the stirring declaration of 1638 came to be thought of as a treaty between Scotland and Heaven, aided by Old Testament associations and no doubt by a conviction that, with God as partner, success was assured. There was an international aspect too, for Calvinism was a creed with adherents in many lands, most of them struggling minorities, many enduring the long ordeal of the Thirty Years War in which thousands of Scottish soldiers were taking part. As the sole country entirely committed to it, Scotland might well feel a special responsibility for its survival; and for Scots to be able to deem themselves a latter-day Chosen People would agreeably feed the national pride, or self-conceit, for which they have come to be known.

In the Assembly at Glasgow in 1638 all the 49 elders who stayed after the king's commissioner Hamilton withdrew were landowners. Of the 86 ministers whose origins are known 34 were sons of ministers; 30 had landed connections, but the majority stood outside the feudal order, and were free of inherited wealth.[16] Evidently there was going to be room for disagreements between lay and clerical in the covenanting ranks. In its social import the Covenant itself was 'essentially conservative'; or, as Gardiner puts it, the noble sponsors were not precisely hypocritical—'they felt strongly in a direction in which it was their interest to feel strongly'.[17] Something of the sort might be said of a great part of human motivation all through history. They wanted an autonomous Scotland under their own sway, an aim they hoped at first to achieve by heading a rebellion against the king, and later by war with England on behalf of a king whom they could now expect to be at their beck and call. Few individuals among them displayed talent, or any lasting principles. One weakness that many of them had in common was that they were head over heels in debt, from trying to live up to English aristocratic standards it may be supposed, and then in the 1640s from expenses and losses inflicted by the wars.

They were very soon dividing into factions. Makey thinks of the quarrel that broke out between Argyll and Montrose as at bottom an old-fashioned feudal one; but his thesis of the effects of inflation suggests something more, a grapple between the feudalism of the west country, more acutely affected by dwindling revenues, and that of the east, less uncomfortably placed and less willing to take the risk of disrupting the old order by damaging its royal figurehead. Aberdeen harboured a school of ecclesiastical thought antithetical to that of the true-blue covenanters. In the west there were cases already in the 1620s of rents 'suddenly and vastly increased', and in 1642 we hear of evictions being threatened.[18] This breach of time-honoured habit might usefully be camouflaged under a parade of religious fervour. The alternative way of escape from financial difficulties, winning of political power, required the backing of the Kirk, or a good part of it; here too zeal was in order.

As to the Kirk, the stirring events that began in 1637 started it into fresh activity, and reawakened its old dream of being hailed as the nation's guide in matters secular as well as spiritual. It was thus led into adventures to which its real resources were quite unequal. With most of its ministers affiliated to classes of the middling sort which were making their way upward, or floating up on the tide of inflation, the Kirk may in a not too fanciful way be pictured as a sort of vanguard of these classes, hoping to achieve along with them a national hegemony. It had undeniably an 'extremist' wing of zealots, some of them doctrinal purists, some stirred by private ambitions, but others with an idealistic trust in their Church's mission.

It may be going too far to say that Johnston of Wariston—or in a different way Laud—'sought the destruction of feudal Scotland'; or that Rutherford, the principal thinker of the movement, was 'planning an assault on the feudal system as such'.[19] Feudalism as a political concept was scarcely yet born. But to the extent that such men were fired by a spirit of change, they must be credited with some purpose, however indistinct, of reorganising the Kirk in order through it to reform the country, and not merely its morals; with some social feeling sympathetic to the masses, even if with few social plans. They were not engrossed in immediate issues alone; for them 1638 was a grand new start, a chance to go back and replace the Kirk as it had grown with the Kirk that ought to have grown. What they wanted in fact was a new Reformation, which would include, or at least imply, resurrection of the hopes of social betterment that had been part of the Kirk's original inspiration.

'This poor, afflicted Kirk had a fine morning, but her night came upon her before her noon-day', Rutherford was writing in 1637. His letters deal with spiritual, not social, salvation; but there may be a hint of something approaching a doctrine of trusteeship in his summons to the Ayrshire Earl of Cassilis to stand forward 'against the mighty of the earth' in defence of the true faith:—'Ye hold your lands of Christ, your charters are under His seal...'[20] Wariston's record in his diary that same year of an ecstatic vision, a sense of divine possession,[21] is in a mystic key very unusual in Calvinist piety; we may make bold to read it as the apocalypse of a new heaven and new earth about to arise in Scotland. And with the official Kirk so much under the thumb of the feudalists, these ardent spirits had no choice but to turn towards the common people: 'extreme radicalism' in Makey's words 'was forced to express itself through the conventicles'.

Scotland was setting off with a flourish towards reasserting itself as the separate kingdom it had lately ceased to be, and returning to the stage of history. Easy early triumphs, due to Charles's embarrassments in England, fanned the mood of confidence. But the story of the following two decades was to be one of incapacity, unrealism, back-stabbing. In 1643 the Solemn League and Covenant bound Scotland and the English parliamentarians together. Its ambiguous title shows theology being substituted for statesmanship. An English presbyterian recorded that Parliament resolved to invite the Scots in as allies because they were 'a wise people, lovers of order, firm to monarchy',—and because it was frightened by the agitation boiling up in London. Before long Levellers were protesting at this reliance on the Scots instead of a full mobilising of English energies. Had it been left to the English people to win its war, the revolution might have gone further, and brought a richer reward.[22]

At the end of 1647 Scottish commissioners entered into an Engagement with the now captive king. Behind it lay alarm among nobles and other conservatives at the prospect of excitement that might be let loose in Scotland by the further spread of radicalism in England. Many Kirk spokesmen were lukewarm and suspicious; the most hostile found a firm base in the south-west. There the united front of 1638 could still in a good measure be maintained. Even among its *seigneurs* some of the most eminent were strong Kirk-and-Covenant men. Shielded by the region's continuing separateness, and lingering clan sentiment, they could feel secure in their ability, hand in hand with the Kirk, to keep the commonalty on the straight and narrow way; they were less easily scared than their fellows elsewhere by the bogy of subversion spreading from England. Men like Cassilis, head of the Kennedy clan, would want to preserve their local importance, and might feel it safest to keep the government—any government—at a distance. Greatest among them was Argyll, eighth Earl and first Marquis, who as chieftain of Clan Campbell was a Highland grandee as well as a Lowland politician, and who was, or posed as (nobody was ever sure which), a presbyterian to the backbone.

There were simmering feelings in the west of a more earthy kind. Makey attributes them to rent increases, now swelling to a climax. He dwells on the 'Mauchline Rising' of June 1648, a brief armed demonstration by 1,000 men, more than half of them mounted and hence to be counted 'men of some substance', led by half a dozen clergymen; this, he writes, showed 'some of the characteristics of a peasants' revolt'. It may be easier to see it as a protest against war burdens which were falling on all Scotland, but which the west might be readiest to resent, like the 'clubmen' in parts of England such as Cornwall. The defeat of the 'Engagers' at Preston in August 1648 spelled opportunity for their opponents. Over-confidence seized the radical Kirk party, as it had seized the whole Kirk at the outset of the civil wars. An armed force from the south-west, recruited mainly from 'the godly of low, but not very low, degree', carried out the *coup d'état* known as the Whiggamore Raid. It was backed by the earls of Cassilis and Eglinton, and Argyll took the lead. Engagers were excluded from office by the Act of Classes in January 1649; the right of lay patrons to nominate ministers was abolished.[23]

It was a declaration of independence by the Kirk, or rather by a minority section opposed by conservatives of all kinds, which had therefore to rely on the lesser landowners and burghers, who in turn felt obliged to seek popular support. Investigation was promised into complaints that war taxes paid by heritors were being passed on by them to their tenants. Feuars were to be free to buy themselves out of further payments.[24] Here were tokens at least of a willingness by the Kirk to turn over a new leaf, or turn back to an old and neglected one; and its staunchest adherents were always to recall this short spell as the finest in its history. Events cut short the experiment, but it may have rekindled some old hopes among common folk.

It must be doubted whether Cromwell and his associates gave much thought to Scottish susceptibilities before resolving to execute Charles, but the effect was calamitous.[25] His forefathers came from Scotland, and to more Scots than Englishmen regicide was sacrilege. Primitive monarchism of a semi-mystic sort was still deeply fixed in the mass mind of Europe. Kirk diehards were weakened, Argyll had to trim his sails, the royalists were soon climbing back into power. In May 1650 they concluded the treaty of Breda with Charles II. In September the Scots army was crushed at Dunbar. A 'Western Association' had been set up, for protection against the English, really also against the Scottish right wing; it had an armed force of its own. In October a Remonstrance was drawn up at Dumfries, urging that the English should be got out of Scotland, but that there should be no further effort to put Charles on the English throne. From now on the Kirk was split between Remonstrants or Protesters, and Engagers or Resolutioners.

If the former were a minority in the country, the latter were so in the south-west, where the throne had never counted for so much as it did closer to the capital. A few noblemen from the west were active royalists. Lists of attendances at meetings of the chief committee in charge of preparations for renewal of war with England show that the most conscientious were Hamilton and the Earl of Galloway, the latter a recent creation who owed his promotion to court favour more than to local standing. Recruiting was obstructed by 'widespread passive resistance', mostly in the west. Argyll had to be reminded that his lands in Lochaber had not provided their quota of men. Glasgow too was recalcitrant, and orders were passed for troops to be quartered on the town until it produced its levy, and for the magistrates to be prosecuted. Detachments from Ulster had hard work to force their way across Galloway. Scotland's best chance now would have been an understanding between the south-west and England, leading on to a new relationship between the two countries. Instead, zealots were bent on recapitulating the follies that the Kirk as a whole had been guilty of since 1638. An officer of their militia, an ardent Protester, attacked an English unit at Hamilton, and suffered a repulse which strengthened the rival wing of the Kirk, until in September the royalist army was destroyed at Worcester.

All through the 1640s national affairs were dominated by war requirements, a field where the Kirk could only play second fiddle, but where its moral influence was vital. Logistics were necessarily clumsy, and the burdens imposed on a poor country were out of all proportion to any gains that could be achieved, once Charles I's teeth had been drawn. Documents edited by David Stevenson show in graphic detail how formidable the problems were; how difficult it was, for instance, with available means of transport, to collect enough grain for an army, even if enough could be got from producers or merchants. Some grain was purloined in transit. There must have been immense profiteering, besides plainer theft. One may wonder how much it added to the accumulation of capital in the hands of the trading class, and to its subsequent progress.

As usual the heaviest burdens fell on the poor. Recruiting was by a form of conscription; Scotland was too poor to employ many troops serving for pay, as England could. Each shire and burgh was called on to raise a levy, and assessed at a cash payment in rough proportion to its resources. A levy might be, as in Lanarkshire in 1648, 'according to the proportion of the fourth man', one in four presumably of able-bodied men available. Some Perthshire estates were ordered to be treated leniently on this occasion, lest, already ravaged by military operations, they should be ruined by lack of tenants.[26] In this way a landowner with influence could earn a claim on the gratitude of his tenantry, as their protector against a call-up.

But the many campaigns, with sometimes three armies on foot, at home and in Ulster and England, meant a terrible drain on the manpower of a country whose population was no more than a million. One consequence must have been a plethora of widows and spinsters, in addition to the always large number of women left unmarried by men emigrating as soldiers or traders. This in turn may help to explain the attachment of women to the Kirk, very striking in the years after 1660. A consolation for men who survived may have been some improvement of conditions due to scarcity of labour.

It was clear to the nobility that it must rely on the Kirk for tutoring the masses, and in particular for getting often reluctant soldiers to do their duty. An Engager acknowledged that his party's charges against Parliament and the English army of hampering religious reforms were false, but necessary— 'without a pretext of religion it is impossible to engage this Kingdom'.[27] A lengthy tirade by Clarendon accuses the Scots leaders of sinking into dependence on the 'senseless and wretched clergy; whose infectious breath corrupted and governed the people, and whose authority was prevalent upon their own [the nobility's] wives'.[28] In 1639 the Scottish camp on Duns Law resounded with preachings and prayers, though also, Baillie admitted, with 'swearing and cursing and brawling in some quarters'.[29] In 1644 when Leslie's army was on the move southward an abundance of sermons was provided, and 'a complete system of ecclesiastical jurisdiction' had been planned, in imitation of procedures in the army of Gustavus Adolphus where

Leslie had served. But he was finding it hard to get chaplains to accompany him; discipline suffered, and Baillie feared that 'our silly simple lads' might be infected by Independent heresies.[30] Presbyteries had to be instructed to find ministers for the expedition. If Notestein is right in blaming Kirk bigotry for a more vindictive and sanguinary temper in the Scottish civil wars than in the English,[31] it may be that some rancour of the Scottish blood-feud, only of late being given up, was finding its way into the pulpit.

Some peasant lads were not as simple as Baillie thought, and by 1651 a good many were absconding, and sometimes selling their horses and weapons. Soldiers, themselves ill-used, were often taxed with molesting and preying on the public.[32] Their being quartered on private houses, even when legal, was a severe infliction; it could be made use of as a mode of coercion, as in 1648 to expedite recruiting in a number of places. Altogether, the penalties of war must have borne more heavily on Scotland than on England, and have ended by making most people anxious for peace at almost any price. Ordinary social oppression was overlaid by the new incubus. Physical exhaustion was compounded by demoralisation from repeated disaster in the field, and the dashing of so many hopes.

After Worcester it was scarcely to be expected that England would leave Scotland alone. A form of union—a kind of shotgun wedding—was insisted on. Once this was completed, English interest declined. Scotland was too poor to be seen as a colony worth exploiting; and there were new wars to be fought, in and out of Europe. Still, while Ireland shows the Commonwealth at its worst, the occupation of Scotland shows it at not far from its best: some of the momentum of progressive ideas stirred up by the civil wars continued there. The English army had a good many grievances of its own, but discipline remained tolerably firm. Early on a colonel was reported to have been suspended and courtmartialled for not putting down theft with enough strictness.[33] But it is hard for any army of occupation to be accepted as a guest, and a large part of the costs fell on Scotland. Those Scots who ought to have recognised the good that could come out of the English presence refused to do so. Isolation helped to reduce the soldiery to a simply professional force; in the end it would be the prime instrument of the Restoration, thus giving back to the Scots the king it had prevented them from winning back.

Kirk leaders of both persuasions had watched developments in England with many misgivings. When Rutherford was in London in 1644 to attend the Westminster Assembly he was distressed to find it swarming with 'Anabaptists, Antinomians, Familists, Separatists'; the least bad, he concluded, were the Independents.[34] Three years later Baillie was horrified at the spectacle of City and Army dictating to Parliament, and felt that with a king at its head Scotland could gather 'the best armie ever we had, for the crushing of these serpents, enemies to God and man'. After Scotland's best army was routed at Dunbar he was disturbed to learn of 'a seed of Hyper-Brownisme', or ultra-sectarianism, sprouting in the minds of some soldiers, who held it 'unlawfull to joyne in armes' with men whose opinions they differed from.[35] Probably the significance of Cromwell's quelling of the English army mutinies in 1647 was lost on most Scots, especially as Leveller agitation was still loud next year, and some of its chiefs were still having to be arrested early in 1649. Their collapse meant that England would not be bringing to Scotland any such thorough programme of reform as it might have done.

Englishmen ruling other countries have always met with much ingratitude. When the Declaration of Union was proclaimed at the mercat cross in Edinburgh in April 1652 a reporter could detect no sign of jubilation: 'soe sencelesse are this generation of theire own goods that scarce a man of them shew'd any signe of rejoycing'. In the heart of the south-west itself, Kirkcudbrightshire rejected the Tender of Incorporation, or union, on the ground that Charles's execution and the overthrow of monarchy violated the terms of the Solemn League and Covenant. It could not be admitted that schismatical England had earned victory by virtue; Scotland's failures must be due to blemishes of its own. Its real sin was its social system and the poverty of the masses; the Kirk preferred to look for it in theological errors or moral backslidings. There was what struck Englishmen as an un-Christian eagerness among Scots to attack one another for 'Adulteries, Incests, and Fornications', and for witchcraft.[36]

Undoubtedly the anti-English sentiment that prevented Scots from making the best of things under the best administration they had ever had was fanned and kept alive largely by the preachers. Among their motives the self-regarding ones cannot be overlooked; 'these fiery Kirkists', a newswriter declared, 'cannot digest a thought of the losse of their infinite power and prerogative'. William Clarke, the army secretary, saw the Kirk in the same jaundiced light when reporting to Speaker Lenthall a conclave of 66 ministers at Edinburgh late in 1651. 'They are much troubled they cannot have that power in civill things... which they were wont to have in this Nation'. As Frances Day comments, all sections of the kirk repudiated any interference by the State, yet all felt that the government ought to be backing them against everyone else.[37]

It was the Protesters whom the occupying authorities felt most desire to encourage, if only because their opponents the Resolutioners persisted in spite of warnings in praying for the king. But narrow-minded dogmatism in the whole Kirk made it greatly to be desired that Scotsmen would begin turning away from presbyterianism towards independent or 'gathered' churches, which would be more friendly to the English connection—very much as the Scots had wanted to see Englishmen turning to presbyterianism. There might then be a realisation that what the 'Godly partie' demanded was 'liberty to tyrannize over the bodies and soules of the poore people under pretence of giving them liberty of conscience'. When the clergy in Perthshire refused to preach unless allowed to pray for the king and his forces, the governor 'said hee would give them leave to preach the gospell of Jesus Christ, but it seems that is not their businesse'.[38] It may not have been too unfair a retort; New Testament ethics were not given a very high place in Scottish teaching.

Poorly attended by chaplains in Ireland, Cromwell had a good number with him in Scotland, and before the end of 1651 Clarke was recommending that more divines should be sent from England, to draw the people away from their 'Pharisaical' cult. This was part of a general strategy, in the early years of the occupation, of undermining the sway of clergy, nobility, gentry, and building on the support of the commonalty, to be won by good government and fair treatment.[39] There was optimism in 1652 over the spread of Independent ideas, largely carried into Scotland by the army. A sermon by an English gospeller at St Giles in Edinburgh came home to its hearers with a force that they acknowledged ' "in their usual way of groans" ': the 'holy groan', as it was called, denoted approval of a preacher's utterances. English officers and soldiers often delivered lay homilies, mounting the pulpit with sword and pistol as if ready, in the words of Hudibras, 'to prove their doctrine orthodox/With apostolic blows and knocks'. To Kirk objections against this usurpation Cromwell replied that the Bible gave no warrant to any claim of a monopoly of truth.[40]

Religious intercourse might do something to broaden Scottish horizons, but in the short run it was likelier to provoke futile wrangling. A great uproar was stirred up against him by Kirk men, George Fox tells us, when he toured Scotland in the autumn of 1657, and they petitioned the authorities to expel him. At one place he came on Friends in great distress, having been excommunicated by 'the Presbyterian priests' and kept from buying anything, even food. No doubt the Kirk often found means of making life uncomfortable for renegades. Baptists whom Fox—as intolerant as any of his adversaries— met were no better; they were 'chaffy, light minds', 'vain janglers and disputers'. Yet he was able to claim some converts, and he foresaw an awakening for Scotland, even though there was such 'abundance of thick, cloddy earth of hypocrisy and falseness' to be dug through.[41] Baillie and his like were horrified at the spread of anarchical notions, and the government's own wish to see sectaries multiplying may well have waned. It was reproached for not giving them sufficient protection.[42] General Monck, in command from 1655, and other army chiefs frowned on Quakerism especially. Some officers were treating their men too much as equals, soldiers might take a dislike to fighting. A sweeping purge of Quakers in the army in Scotland was carried out in 1657.

By dragging a reluctant Scotland back into war with England in 1650-51, and then being beaten, the nobility got itself into a highly vulnerable position. There could have been no better occasion for putting an end to its mischief-making for good. One aim of what may be called a 'defeudalising' programme (as again in the Highlands after 1746) was to make it harder for the lords to rebel by freeing the masses from their power, which, Parliament believed, enabled them to coerce tenants or clansmen into joining them.[43] Cultivators were to be relieved of bond-services and feudal vassalage. To carry agrarian reform further would have been a difficult and complicated task, for which the men in charge of Scotland had no leisure; moreover it would have stimulated inconvenient calls for similar reforms in England.

Even so, the measures taken, and others talked of or feared, were quite enough to alarm the feudal camp, and make it ready to listen to the propaganda kept steadily going by Charles and his advisers. An address to 'the Nobles and Gentlemen of Scotland', dated June 1656, warned them that the purpose of English 'insolence and tyranny' was 'the extirpation of the ancient Nobility and Gentry'. It was less easy for royalists to strike the right note with the Kirk; and as Hyde ruefully said, it was hard to know how to draw up a comprehensive manifesto, because the Kirk could not be left out, but what could be said that would satisfy it? This dilemma pointed forward to the determination shown after 1660 to put the Kirk in a straitjacket. It was shared by the English, who discovered that some 'Malignants' were readier than any of the ministers to welcome the union, out of detestation of everything presbyterian.[44]

In the story of the occupation the critical turning-point came with the royalist rising of 1653-55. It was a revolt of disgruntled lords, only strong enough to make a fight of it in the Highlands, but capable of raiding far and wide from their lair, and setting off small disturbances here and there; thanks to anti-English prejudice they could count on at least tacit support nearly everywhere. Troops marching north were harassed by countryfolk removing supplies from their path, and 'stragglers were snapped up'. It was a rebellion very much like those of 1715 and 1745, though on a more limited scale. A feature common to all three was the indebtedness of many landowners and chiefs, driving them to desperation. They were nearly all in a parlous condition, Baillie heard, sinking under the weight of their debts and fines.[45] Whether or not there was any political calculation behind this, the courts under official instructions had been enforcing the penalties against debtors much more severely than in the past. A bigger English army could have put the trouble-makers down in short order, but Colonel Robert Lilburne, in command until replaced by Monck, kept having to expostulate, with little response from London, about his forces being inadequate, and starved of equipment and sometimes of pay. England was at war with Holland from 1652 to 1654. He felt compelled to halt and even reverse any drive against feudalism by telling judges to treat debtors—the Earl of Mar, for instance—more gently, so as not to push them into throwing in their lot with the rebels.[46]

Disoriented and divided as it was, the Kirk's attitude could only be ambivalent. It could have little love for the Malignants, yet a king might be a lesser evil than toleration and its brood of sects. Ministers of the 'Assembly partie', or majority, Lilburne wrote in April 1653, when the outbreak was looming up, 'cease nott to blowe the trumpett to prepare the people for something they themselves do nott well understand'. In July he thought proper to nip a meeting of the General Assembly in the bud, for fear of collusion with the rebels; the Protester faction seemed pleased, but he was not sure of them either.[47] As the rebellion dragged on he blamed the Kirk for much of the grassroots sympathy it seemed to be getting. Support for the government was disappointingly meagre; this must have been one cause of the retreat from the early plan of relying on the people against their masters, and from measures which the feudal revolt really ought to have accelerated. Fines and confiscation of royalist estates imposed after the English entry were gradually whittled down.[48] In similar style during the Indian Mutiny a century later the British began with threats to expropriate the great landlords of Oudh, and finished by pardoning and reinstating them. If history ever repeats itself monotonously, it is in the field of empire.

One of the five Cromwellian forts in Scotland was built in 1652 at Ayr; the attack on the English troops not far away in the previous year had clearly not been forgotten. In the following years the south-west was falling, like the English government, into a more and more isolated position; the fact ought to have drawn them together, but did not. Attitudes here to the union were very mixed. In the country as a whole, out of 89 constituencies called on to declare their opinion, 70 accepted incorporation (too high a figure to be really representative), only 3 rejected it, including Glasgow and Kirkcudbright; 16 took no part, among them 11 shires or burghs of the west or south-west, 4 of these abstaining on the ground of poverty. On the other hand all but one of the constituencies displaying positive cordiality also belonged to the west or south-west.[49] These anomalies may reflect divergences of local interests, and for some areas a growing attractiveness of English markets. In terms of Kirk politics there was more homogeneity, and Lilburne took comfort from the ascendancy of the Protesters. 'The people in the west', he wrote in April 1653, 'who have bin alwayes accounted most precise' (rigid, dogmatic), were showing signs of coming round, and if won over 'would bee the most confiding people in this Nation'.[50]

He was unpleasantly surprised a year later by a royalist rising in Dumfriesshire and Galloway. It was a small affair, and like the rebellion in the north essentially feudal. Luckily Argyll stood by the government, embroidering his loyalty with stiltedly pious protestations of the sort that everyone in those days, from Cromwell and Charles II down, had to learn. He was 'almost drowned with debt', according to Baillie, 'in friendship with the English, but in hatred with the country' from his recent tergiversations. His son and heir Lord Lorne by contrast was a royalist partisan, though not much trusted, Baillie thought, by his leaders, any more than his father was by Lilburne. Lorne's chief local ally was the fourth Viscount Kenmure, who stood out in equally strong contrast with the Kenmure who died in 1634 denouncing Laudian rituals as 'idolatrous and antichristian', devices of popery and hell.[51] Dissensions of that age, in the upper classes, can sometimes look like animosities between generations.

By themselves such malcontents were not dangerous, but even here in the south-west they seemed to have some backing. Protesters might sound as if they detested Kenmure and his disorderly following, when Lilburne talked to them, but he feared that even a minor attack on his soldiers could ignite 'the spiritt of the generality of people here, who have a deadly antipathy against us'.[52] Had the region come under heavier pressure from the rebels, the Protesters might have been obliged to take sides with England. As it was, they were sheltered by the English forces, and could afford to go on hugging a self-complacent, self-righteous neutrality, along with a high-toned reliance on Heaven and its pledges to its chosen people.

Restoration in 1660 brought Scotland a nominal divorce from England, a separation that from now on meant very little. There was a second Privy Council again, but its nucleus worked in London, with English assessors, much as Aragon was governed by a Council of Aragon at Madrid. For local administration Justices of the Peace were instituted afresh, and lairds thus given a bigger sphere; but the Act which commissioned them in 1661 reserved to those entitled to them—chiefly the greater landowners—all 'rights priviledges and liberties' granted by the Crown.[53] Seigneurial dues swept away by the English were restored. A shift from land revenue to indirect taxation was a more substantial gift to the nobility. Chastened by hard experience, it was being allowed a junior partnership with the aristocracy restored to power in England. It was to show, as Makey says, 'a remarkable capacity to adjust itself to the underlying changes of the period'; superiors and vassals were merging in a common class of heritors.[54]

They were aided by a recovery of rents, part of an all-round economic improvement brought about by the return of peaceful conditions, and closer association with England. The more central areas of the country were moving in a modern direction. There was intellectual development in the later seventeenth century, and from the 1670s trade and industries were giving signs of growth. This benefited primarily the burghs, which Monck—more clear-sighted than Lilburne with his hopes of the south-west—had singled out as the sector of Scottish life most amicable to England. But there was some amelioration even for the peasant in his hovel; his diet was coming to be as a rule adequate though monotonous.[55]

The first hundred years of the Kirk had led to frustration and schism. Vaulting ambition had o'erleaped itself, and it was in no shape now to resist the settlement imposed on it in 1662. The government was popular, the Kirk was not—one reason for which must have been its close association with so much warfare, and the burden of conscription, and the sacrifices of the battlefield. Its form of worship was not interfered with; but bishops came back, and ministers had to take an oath of allegiance and be presented by a patron. By way of a cheap sweetener, J.P.s and their constables were directed to prevent any profanation of the Sabbath. There was no choice but discreet conformism, or expulsion.

Episcopacy, or 'Erastianism', was the great stumbling-block. Prelacy had for long been vituperated as popery in disguise, and well-founded suspicions of the leanings of Charles and his brother to Rome were to keep this feeling alive. In vain moderates like Leighton proposed a blend of moderate episcopacy and presbyterianism, somewhat as in James I's later years. Charles II's men were to be real bishops, with real teeth and claws for use in their master's service. They would be 'performing functions locally as royal, judicial and financial servants', and providing a reliable platoon in Parliament. There was still not much of a bureaucracy for the king to rule through, and no regular standing army, though troops would be mobilised when required, and a militia was to be set up as an armed police. After all their tribulations, Charles and his henchmen might well feel nervous, the more so with a Scotland full of men with military experience.

Many Resolutioners, as well as Protesters, refused to submit to the new dispensation, and their best men declined offers of bishoprics. Between a third and a quarter of the total number of ministers stood out; they were most numerous, predictably, in the west. Some went further and defied the order to quit their parishes. Such open defiance, accompanied by illegal conventicling, was chiefly though not entirely confined to the west. Official reactions over the next quarter-century wavered between coercion and conciliation, each in turn failing to yield the hoped-for results in face of what the exasperated Lauderdale, Secretary for Scotland, called 'a peevish, wilful, and an unsatisfiable generation'.[56]

During spells of cruder resort to force, the south-west was treated, as Scotland had not been by Cromwell, as a conquered territory. A 'Highland Host' sent to terrorise the area in 1678 'ran wild and plundered and destroyed indiscriminately'. It was a presage of much future use of Highland troops, in rather more orderly style, for imperial operations abroad. Another exceptional factor was Ulster, which could be a refuge for Covenanters but was also a nursery of heavy-handed *conquistadores*. It is pointed out by Patricia Wilson, in her notes to *Ringan Gilhaize*, that a number of commanders in these Scottish broils had served in Ulster; among them the leader of the Pentland Rising, Colonel Wallace, but there were more individuals on the government side, like the brutal persecutors Turner and Dalziel. Here again was an omen of much colonial history to come. There may well have been common soldiers too in action against the Covenanters who had learned their trade in the bloody pacification of Ulster.[57]

Despite all this, dissent was never suffocated, though it was increasingly penned up in one corner of Scotland, condemned from 1638 to 1688 to go through a half-century of turmoil and suffering. It was a nearly unique case of prolonged religious strife over matters not of creed but of church government. Yet the Covenant of 1638 was a pledge to defend the faith, and made no direct allusion to episcopacy. It must have been the eviction of their pastors, fathers of the people in their own parishes, that turned many ordinary folk into dissenters; in their persons we can suppose the Kirk to have displayed the social sympathies that as an organisation it failed to make manifest. Himself a son of the manse, Lockhart wrote eloquently of how for a devout presbyterian 'the image of his minister and the idea of his superior sanctity' took the place of all Catholic or Anglican ceremony, and how in times of persecution they could be regarded as 'nothing less than so many moveable tabernacles', the visible embodiment of the Kirk in the wilderness.[58] They were abandoning all worldly gear, resigning themselves to apostolic poverty. Such men were well fitted to be the guides of an ill-nourished peasantry; they and it were undergoing the same painful pilgrimage.

It is understandable that the veneration in which these pastors were held— only conceivable in such an out of the way, behind-the-times, region— provoked very different views of them in many others. They were grave and sober men, in Gilbert Burnet's estimation, with little learning other than scriptural, their prayers lengthy, their preaching plain but 'very dull'.[59] A modern writer finds fault with Alexander Peden, a survivor of the Pentland Rising and five years imprisonment on the Bass Rock, for 'ferocity and intolerance', even though he did not belong to the Cameronian wing.[60]

Bigger landowners in the south-west were not in general hostile, or willing to help in the work of repression. There were divergences of outlook among them, along with ramifying family links outside as well as within the province. About the time when Charles I and Scotland came to blows, the pious Lord Kenmure had a cousin married to the provost of Kirkcudbright, while his wife was a sister of the Marquis of Argyll, so that his successor in the 1650s and the latter's fellow-royalist Lord Lorne were kinsmen. Sundry peerages were of quite recent creation, like the earldoms of Wigtown, Dumfries, and Nithsdale, bestowed on holders of old 'baronies', or well-off lairds. An Earl of Wigtown was first cousin to Montrose.[61] Something of an old patriarchal relation between landlord and peasantry might subsist in this secluded region. A nobleman of the old breed like Cassilis had a special standing in the community that no ruler could bestow, and to retain its respect he could not bend overmuch to the government, or let himself be made its agent for bullying his humble neighbours.

Men like him were not prepared to embark on any fresh Whiggamore Raids. In the two risings, one starting from an incident at Dalry in Galloway, followed by an occupation of Dumfries and a march on Edinburgh, the other spreading from Ayrshire to Glasgow, it may be permissible to see the spirit of the minor lairds of the south-west at work. Those who joined in were taking up the hoary tradition of rebellion that the magnates were abandoning. In the 1666 foray its quick advance, and its finding leaders outside its birthplace, may suggest some previous planning. Any such challenge was the more perturbing to the authorities because of fears, as in Ireland, of foreign meddling. Presbyterians in both Scotland and England had some contacts with Holland.

It was in Ayrshire and Galloway, on the humblest plane of society above the floating mass of vagrants or ne'er-do-weels—the peasantry and those closest to it, like village artisans—that the cause was most tenaciously upheld. Passive resistance was their choice, a dogged resolve not to give in, but to bear witness steadily and wait for the better days that Heaven must some day reward them with. In the meantime what they endured could not fail to convince every man or woman of their election. Sometimes they might almost seem to be inviting harassment, by way of purgation (fasting was a favourite ritual of those times), as other devotees have worn hairshirts or slept on beds of nails. They gave good evidence of a capacity for organisation, which presbyterian practices as well as neighbourhood spirit must have encouraged, and army service may have strengthened. At parish level, ordinary folk had been acquiring a place in the kirk sessions, a voice in local affairs which they would not want to be deprived of by a meddlesome bishop. Conventicling, the habit of unofficial, even anti-official, religious gatherings, had long been familiar; Cowan suggests that 'conventicling' would be a more appropriate name for what was happening now than covenanting.[62]

A forbidden gathering out in the wilds was necessarily a more democratic affair than a formal service in church. The upheavals of the years before 1660 had shaken the old docility of the lower orders, and given these people courage to defy both Church and State; but they had not supplied them with ideas that could enable them to move forward. It does not appear that the social-reforming mood of the radical Kirk in the late 1640s survived into this final phase. Rutherford, Wariston, Guthrie, were dead. There is little sign of any similar breadth of vision in men like Peden. Their followers were as unquestioningly faithful to the Lord of Hosts as they had been in not much earlier days to their clan-lords. This, as well as the protection that some landowners were ready to give them against the government's myrmidons, restrained the peasantry from social protest. Whatever may have been the case with symptoms of discontent during the 1640s, it does not appear that social unrest—except at several removes or translations—can explain the covenanters. Had it been strong or distinct enough it would surely have pierced through the veil of theology, instead of thickening it. Relegated to the wilderness, the radical Kirk movement turned into its opposite, a conservative clinging to the past.

The lack of active support for the two risings outside their own bounds is a measure of the widening gap between the south-west and the rest of the country. Covenanters were left to play the part of a dogged rearguard, holding fast to vows once deemed sacred by the whole nation. They could contemplate themselves, in Old Testament style, as protagonists in a stupendous drama, a cosmic cataclysm, and the rest of the Kirk as so many worshippers of Baal. 'O Heavens', wrote one of them (in a small house on the Winterhope Burn in the Borders, Hogg says), 'be astonished at this, and horribly afraid! for *Scotland* hath changed her Glory... by an unparalleled Apostasie'.[63] While in more 'progressive' areas, drifting towards capitalist landowning and industry, class division was being more openly exposed, in Galloway a vestige of the fraternal temper of 1638 could linger on.

It was this unity, perhaps, that the covenanters were really trying to keep alive, the solidarity of a local community—only expressible by them in very abstract forms—in danger of crumbling in the air of a new age. For a society in distress, to hold on to a creed for which many had given their lives was the best way of holding on to the past; it was a refusal to admit that times were changing, because God's will could not change. The Kirk's own distresses made it a suitable image of a time-honoured way of life approaching its end. Its faithful pastors, an ageing remnant, were a memorial of better days. Mostly of respectable birth, they had, Burnet observed, 'so great an interest both with the gentry and commonalty that it was no wonder if the turning out so many all at once made great impressions on them'.[64] A prayer-meeting on a wild moor, with sentries posted round, could hardly be surpassed as an event to inspire an intense feeling of mutual trust, a sense of oneness that could concentrate into an hour the consciousness of a whole generation.

Few pastors were willing to sanction resort to arms, except in immediate self-defence. Many of their disciples were straining at the leash; they became the 'Cameronians' or adherents of Richard Cameron, killed in a skirmish in 1680. Liberation came in the end from England, or the Whig grandees to whom the lowly name of Whiggamore descended, and the Prince of Orange; but it found hundreds ready to hail it and unsheath their swords. This was a brief explosion of energy, quickly dissipated, and leaving the old guard of the movement little further to do or to hope for. They bequeathed to their native hills a political spirit which could be roused afresh by accidents of history. The Jacobites retreating from Derby in 1745, writes Petrie, 'marched by Dumfries to Glasgow, through a countryside that for generations had been notoriously hostile to the Prince's ancestors'.[65] Glasgow was so refractory— as in 1648—that it was made to pay a forced contribution to his funds.

The later covenanters offer a rare example of a class near the bottom of society holding grimly to a creed constructed by intellectuals of higher ranks, when most of the propertied were turning away from it. These Galloway rustics learned to reason acutely, but only within the limits of a world bounded by the Shorter Catechism. They could only float up into the clouds of theology, or sink into doctrinal quicksands deeper than any of their bogs. Staunch believers in predestination, they were in the grip of a destiny of another kind, fashioned for them by all Scotland's past history. A class with no future, or only one of painful struggle for survival, was defending the dead letter of a treaty with God as its last anchorage, holding aloft a banner with a strange device whose meaning it had forgotten.

Some have thought of the covenanters as 'part of a wider phenomenon', champions like many others of conservative thinking against innovation and modernity; the Old Believers in seventeenth-century Russia offer an analogy.[66] They suggest comparisons also with the later days of the sects, offspring of the revolution, in England. Among these were the Quakers, retiring into a moral philosophy with a lively social conscience and finding some of their converts in the quietist atmosphere of Aberdeen. In southern France at the end of the century the Camisards, the Protestant peasantry of the Cevennes, were waging desperate war against both inquisitors and tax-collectors. Onlookers were struck by their superstitious practices, their prophesyings, convulsions, miracles, and it was the same with the short-lived sect of 'Camisars', their offshoot in England.[67] The men of the Cevennes had objectives in part very rational, but they were engaged in a war dreadfully barbarous, and needed the stimulus of something more primitive, more magical, than Calvinism. Such hysteria was seldom observed among the covenanters, but a touch of it can be recognised in their belief in the strange gifts that gave Peden his title of 'the Prophet', as if he had been the Merlin who once haunted those same hills, reborn.

One more variant of peasant action unfolded itself very close to Galloway, in Cumbria. There, from the later sixteenth century to the late eighteenth, tenants with occupancy rights sanctioned by custom were combining, on one estate or another, against the attempts of lords of manors to increase feudal fines and practice other means of exploitation. Through all the long period the tenants achieved at least partial success, sometimes resorting to mild forms of direct action, more often by getting the courts to sustain their claims. In 1723 those on the Percy estates entered into their own businesslike version of a covenant—a 'Strict and Solemn Combination and Confederacy... to stand by and assist each other with Mutual Contributions'.[68]

To Voltaire, looking back from the Age of Reason on the fanaticism and strife he thought peculiar to Christianity, Scottish presbyterianism appeared 'a kind of republicanism whose pedantry and austerity were even more intolerable than the severity of the climate', a scourge only checked at last by 'reason, laws and force'. Good sense has not been the only, probably not the strongest motor of progress; there has also been needed an ingredient, a yeast, of heroic folly. Very much of history has been a squandering of idealism and devotion in the service of irrational or hopeless causes, or worse. Yet the late covenanters were displaying qualities without which humanity can have no future. They defended principles against a bad government. R.L. Stevenson honoured their disdain for convention, *respectability*—'what the Covenanters used to call 'rank conformity': the deadliest gag and wet blanket that can be laid on men'.[69]

Another of many later men and women who felt their spell was Charlotte Bronte's heroine Shirley, very much an early feminist, who had daydreams of adventures, perils, of going on crusade, or 'following a covenanting captain up into the hills to hold a meeting out of reach of persecuting troopers', with battle, it might be, as the sequel to prayer.[70]

NOTES

1. E.C. Mossner, *The Life of David Hume* (Edinburgh, 1954), 13, 33.
2. J.G. Lockhart, *Peter's Letters to his Kinsfolk* (abbreviated edn., London, 1952), Letters 29 and 34.
3. In *Tales and Sketches*, ed. D.O. Hill (Glasgow, 1837). This contains also a short story about covenanter fugitives, 'A Tale of Pentland'.
4. R. and K.M. Lizars, *In the Days of the Canada Company... 1825-1850* (Toronto, 1896), 46.
5. I.B. Cowan, 'The covenanters. A revision article', *Scottish Historical Review*, XLVII, (1968), 37.
6. W. Thompson, 'The Kirk and the Cameronians', in *Rebels and their Causes*, ed. M. Cornforth (London, 1978), 98-9.
7. See *The Party-Coloured Mind...*, ed. David Reid (Edinburgh, 1982), 172.
8. Walter Makey, *The Church of the Covenant...* (Edinburgh, 1979), 5, 167. T.C. Smout, *A History of the Scottish People* (London, 1972), chap. 6, draws a less favourable picture of tenures and tenants' security. For the references to Smout above, see *ibid.*, 129-30, 114.
9. 'Heathercat', in R.L. Stevenson, *Lay Morals and Other Papers* (London, 1920), 301.
10. *The Government of Scotland under the Covenanters 1637-1651*, ed. David Stevenson (Edinburgh, 1982), 45; C.H. Firth, *Scotland and the Commonwealth. Letters and papers...* (Edinburgh, 1895), 170-1; on the burghs cf. Stevenson, *The Scottish Revolution 1637-1644* (Newton Abbot, 1973), 27, 51, 308-9.
11. For the quotations and references in this paragraph, see Makey, *The Church of the Covenant*, 1, 6, 181, 4, 12, 173.
12. *Ibid.*, 37-8.
13. P. Collinson, *The Religion of Protestants. The Church in English Society, 1559-1625* (Oxford, 1982), chap. 4.
14. G. Donaldson, *Scotland, James V-James VII* (Edinburgh, 1978), 302.
15. Collinson, *The Religion of Protestants*, 270-1. Patricia Wilson, in notes to *Ringan Gilhaize* (Edinburgh, 1984), 329, 340, remarks that 'Covenant' and similar terms were often used loosely and indiscriminately.
16. Makey, *The Church of the Covenant*, 46-7; cf. 96.
17. D. Stevenson, *Revolution and Counter-Revolution in Scotland, 1644-1651* (London, 1977), 232; S.R. Gardiner, *History of England 1603-1642* (London, 1884), vol.8, 313.
18. Makey, *The Church of the Covenant*, 168-71.
19. *Ibid.*, 19, 54.
20. *Letters of Samuel Rutherford*, ed. A.B. Bonar (Edinburgh, 1863), vol.1, 453; vol.2, 190.
21. Reid, *The Party-Coloured Mind*, 41-3.
22. *The Good Old Cause*, ed. C. Hill and E. Dell (London, 1949), 296-7; Makey, *The Church of the Covenant*, 69, 71 argues oppositely that English dislike of dependence on a foreign army hastened the creation of the New Model, and thus pushed the revolution forward.
23. *Ibid.*, 75, 174, 177.
24. *Ibid.*, 80-1; Stevenson, *Revolution and Counter-Revolution*, 213.
25. For these paragraphs see *Ibid.*, 108; and his *The Government of Scotland*, 168-9, 71, 79-80, 140.
26. *Ibid.*, 68, 69.
27. Stevenson, *Revolution and Counter-Revolution*, 103-4.

28. *Selections from Clarendon*, ed. G. Huehns (Oxford, 1978), 303-4.
29. Reid, *The Party-Coloured Mind*, 63.
30. C.H. Firth, *Cromwell's Army* (London, 1902), 315-17.
31. W. Notestein, *The Scot in History*, 144.
32. Stevenson, *Revolution and Counter-Revolution*, 121, 141 (cf. 16, 65), 91 (cf. 96).
33. Firth, *Cromwell's Army*, 294.
34. *Letters of Samuel Rutherford*, vol.2, 314.
35. *The Letters and Journals of Robert Baillie*, ed. D. Laing (Edinburgh, 1842), vol.3, 9, 126-7.
36. Firth, *Scotland and the Commonwealth*, 41, 367-9 (cf. Smout, *History of the Scottish People*, 77).
37. For this paragraph see F.D. Dow, *Cromwellian Scotland 1651-1660* (Edinburgh, 1979), 29, 204; Firth, *Scotland and the Commonwealth*, 336 (cf. 339); G.D. Henderson, *Church and Ministry. A Study in Scottish Experience* (London, 1951), 67.
38. Firth, *Scotland and the Commonwealth*, 33, 6-7.
39. Dow, *Cromwellian Scotland*, 27, 52; Firth, *Scotland and the Commonwealth*, 15 n.2, quotes the Welsh regicide Colonel John Jones: 'It is the interest of the Commonwealth of England to break the interest of the great men in Scotland...'
40. Firth, *Cromwell's Army*, 324-5, 338.
41. *The Journal of George Fox* (London, 1924), 154-63.
42. Firth, *Scotland and the Commonwealth*, xl-xli.
43. Dow, *Cromwellian Scotland*, 31-2.
44. Firth, *Scotland and the Commonwealth*, 46, 259-61, xxvi-xxvii.
45. *The Letters... of ... Baillie*, vol.3, 255, 249, 288.
46. Firth, *Scotland and the Commonwealth*, 239; cf. 266, 271-2, 289, 296.
47. *Ibid.*, 122-3, 162-3.
48. Dow, *Cromwellian Scotland*, 56, 58.
49. *Ibid.*, 40-2.
50. Firth, *Scotland and the Commonwealth*, 126-7; cf. Julia Buckroyd, *Church and State in Scotland 1660-1681* (Edinburgh, 1980), 10-11.
51. *The Letters ... of ... Baillie*, vol.3, 249-50; D. Matthew, *Scotland under Charles I*, 36ff.
52. Firth, *Scotland and the Commonwealth*, 271; cf. 273, 275.
53. *The Acts of the Parliament of Scotland, 1424-1707* (2nd edn., London, 1966), 82-5.
54. Makey, *The Church of the Covenant*, 64, 185.
55. Dow, *Cromwellian Scotland*, 148; Smout, *History of the Scottish People*, 142.
56. For the above two paragraphs, and the beginning of the next, see Buckroyd, *Church and State...*, 46, 99, 127.
57. Outrages attributed to Scottish troops in Ulster are detailed by Thomas Fitzpatrick, *The Bloody Bridge... the Insurrection of 1641* (Dublin, 1903), 150ff.
58. Lockhart, *Peter's Letters...*, Letter 29.
59. Reid, *The Party-Coloured Mind*, 124-5.
60. C.B.H. Cant, 'The archpriest Avvakum and his Scottish Contemporaries', *Slavonic and East European Review*, vol.44 (1965-66), 391, 396. I owe this reference to Professor Paul Dukes.
61. Matthew, *Scotland Under Charles I*, 38, 106, 297.
62. For the above two paragraphs, see Buckroyd, *Church and State...*; Makey, *The Church of the Covenant*, 104, 148-9; Cowan, 'The Covenanters...', 46.
63. Alexander Shields, *A Hind let loose* (1st edn., 1687), 97.
64. Reid, *The Party-Coloured Mind*, 125.

65. Sir Charles Petrie, *The Jacobite Movement. The Last Phase 1716-1807* (London, 1950), 103-4.
66. Paul Dukes, *October and the World: Perspectives on the Russian Revolution* (London, 1979), 6.
67. J. Murray, *Life in Scotland a Hundred Years Ago* (Paisley, 1900), 182.
68. C.E. Searle, 'The Cumbrian Customary Economy in the Eighteenth Century', *Past and Present*, Feb. 1986, no.110.
69. Voltaire, *The Age of Louis XIV* (London, 1961), chap. 36; Stevenson, *Lay Morals*, 41.
70. Charlotte Bronte, *Shirley* (1849), chap.17.

3 THE COVENANTING TRADITION AND SCOTTISH RADICALISM IN THE 1790s[1]

John Brims

Students of modern Scottish history do not have to delve very deeply into their subject before becoming aware of the importance of the covenanters as a source of inspiration and legitimation for the activities of various movements which have sought to bring about radical change in Scotland. The appeal to and identification with the covenanting tradition is a motif which runs through the modern history of the Scottish people. It can be traced back from the home rule national covenant of 1949 to the Red Clydesiders of the 1920s, the chartists of 1838-1848, the political unions of 1831-1832, and the radicals of 1816-1820. Was the covenanting tradition an invention of nineteenth-century radicalism, or, to put the question in a different way, can the tradition be traced back further, to the Friends of the People and the United Scotsmen of the 1790s?

While W.L. Mathieson was almost certainly guilty of exaggeration in claiming that the 'lower orders' of late eighteenth-century Scotland were 'prepared to welcome the theocracy as well as the theology of the Covenant', there can be no doubt that, in the lowlands at least, they were still strictly Calvinist in their theology and strongly attached to the memory of the covenanters. In the Ayrshire of the 1780s, for example, the covenanting tradition was still alive, and of the covenanters, who had opposed

> the agents of oppression under what was called emphatically the bloody house of Stuart, ... interesting anecdotes derived from a comparatively fresh tradition were told ... around the evening fire, by the old, in the audience of the young, thus creating, or deepening a salutary horror of persecution for conscience sake, as well as strong prepossessions in favour of true religion, of holy courage, and of steadfast suffering for the sake of righteousness and vital godliness.[2]

The tradition was probably at its strongest in Ayrshire and Lanarkshire, but it was not limited to west central Scotland. In 1790 a French visitor remarked that 'all the polemical divinity and enthusiastic notions of the last century continue to be retailed among the believing multitude', adding that 'a religious fervour burns throughout the whole nation and ingrosses every other passion'.[3] A decade later the *Scots Magazine* commented that the Scots 'peasantry' were characterised both by a taste for 'controversial divinity', which helped to keep alive their 'fanatical spirit' and develop their 'polemical acuteness', and by an excessive veneration for 'the same religious books which inflamed the zeal of their forefathers' and were 'connected with many traditional anecdotes of the piety of their ancestors'.[4] George Robertson recalled in 1829 that the farmers of pre-improvement Scotland held 'similar principles' to those of the covenanters, venerated their practices, read Samuel Rutherford, and 'had a taste for ancient histories connected with their country, as ... Pentland-Hills, and Drumclog, and Bothwell Brig', and that the cottars of that period 'also were of covenanting descent, and had books of a similar tendency with those of their masters, but on a lesser scale, being usually pamphlets or religious tracts, such as ... *The Hind let Loose*'.[5]

The covenanting tradition was upheld most strongly within the tiny Reformed Presbyterian (Cameronian) Church and the much more numerous Secession Church which in 1744 had split into what became popularly known as the Burgher and Antiburgher Synods. Until the advent of the 'new light' controversy in the closing years of the century, both branches of the Secession adhered to the testimony of 1734 which acknowledged 'the perpetual obligation of the National Covenant, frequently sworn by all ranks of persons in Scotland, [and] also of the Solemn League and Covenant sworn by all ranks both in England and Scotland'.[6] The desire of the seceders 'to adhere to the principles of the true presbyterian covenanted Church of Scotland'[7] was reflected by the agreement in 1742 to renew the Covenants and by the decision two years later to make the Covenants a term of communion.[8] The rigidly conservative doctrine of the Secession did not inhibit its growth during the second half of the century of enlightenment, and by the 1790s contemporaries were estimating the number of its adherents at between 100,000 and 150,000.[9] If the latter figure is accepted as roughly accurate, then the seceders accounted for as much as 10 per cent of the population of the country. Whatever the exact figure, there can be no doubt that the seceders constituted a large and, in the circumstances of the 1790s, politically significant minority. An examination of the response of the seceders to the issues raised by the French Revolution and the subsequent campaign for radical parliamentary reform in Britain would therefore help to establish whether or not the covenanting tradition had a political as well as a religious validity in late eighteenth-century Scotland.

The British government and its supporters in the 1790s had no difficulty in identifying the political principles of the seceders. In their eyes, every seceder was guilty of 'Jacobinism' until proved innocent. For example, Lord Advocate Robert Dundas wrote to his uncle Henry Dundas, the Secretary of State for War and government 'manager' of Scotland, in October 1794 stating that 'all that Description of Clergy and their Hearers are deeply disaffected',[10] while in July of the same year the ultra-conservative Sir William Murray of Ochtertyre informed the Duke of Atholl that in drawing up an assessment of the political sympathies of people living in his district 'all dissenters' except those known personally to be loyal 'will be marked *S*' for suspected democrat.[11] This view of the seceders' politics requires considerable qualification. In 1795 some of the leading dissenting clergy volunteered to spy upon the 'factious' for Lord Advocate Dundas,[12] while the Secession provided two of the most able conservative pamphleteers of the period in John Young (1743-1806), the Antiburgher minister of Hawick, and Alexander Shanks (1732-1799), the Burgher minister of Jedburgh.[13] It is significant, however, that the government informers were employed to spy upon members of their own churches, and that pamphleteers of a conservative turn of mind tended to run into trouble with both their congregations and their church courts. 'Mr Young, of Hawick ... was punished by an almost total Desertion of his Auditory', Lord Advocate Dundas complained, 'and no pains [were] spared to vilify and libel his Character both Religious and Political'.[14] In October 1794 it was reported that 'Mr Young is likely to be seriously attacked by the Antiburgher Judicatures' and that that attack was being prepared by the presbytery of Forfar who had appointed a committee to investigate his pamphlet.[15] The meeting of the Antiburghers' General Synod in May 1795 saw a formal complaint presented against Young charging him with having advanced opinions in his *Essays on Government* inconsistent with the testimony of the Synod. A three man committee, which included two well-known supporters of the radical reform movement in Archibald Bruce and James Robertson, was appointed to determine whether the complaint was well-founded,[16] but in the event no further proceedings were taken against Young. It seems clear that the Young case gravely embarrassed the General Associate Synod. They would have realised that any disciplinary action against Young would have appeared to outsiders, including an alarmist and ruthlessly repressive government, as tantamount to a statement of support for the radical reformers, and would therefore have concluded that the best policy was to keep the threat of disciplinary action hanging over Young's head[17] without doing anything to antagonise government by implementing it. Having 'growled at the pamphlet',[18] the Antiburghers prudently refrained from trying to bite its author.

While Young's implicit attack upon the covenanted testimony of his own church would have outraged virtually the whole Synod, at least some of its members would also have been upset by its uncompromising defence of the old regime and its criticism of the reform movement. At least three ministers of the Antiburgher church served as delegates to the Scottish radical reformers' national conventions. John Wilson (1733-1803) of Methven, one of 'the leading men' of the Perth association of the Friends of the People,[19] was delegated to the first convention in December 1792,[20] while James Robertson (1750-1811) and Frederick McFarlane of Kilmarnock and Montrose respectively served as delegates to the second convention in April 1793.[21] Moreover, James McEwan (c.1750-1813), the Antiburgher minister of Dundee, attended a meeting of the radical Society for Constitutional Information in London on 11 April 1794[22] and was, around the same time, elected by the Dundee Friends of Liberty as their delegate to the proposed second British convention.[23]

Turning our attention to the other branch of the Secession, the Burghers, a similar level of involvement in radical politics may be observed. Dr George Lawson (1749-1820), the Burgher Professor of Divinity and minister of

Selkirk, William Kidston (c.1728-1808), the minister of Stow, and Ebenezer Hislop (1746-1831), the minister of Shotts, were named in a correspondence list[24] probably drawn up in late 1793 by William Skirving (died 1796), a former student at the Burgher theological college[25] and *de facto* national secretary of the Scottish Friends of the People. The specific purpose of this list is not clear, although it may have served as a list of those whom Skirving wished to inform of the arrival of the English delegates to the British Convention in early November 1793 and of the decision to recall the Scottish delegates. Whatever the precise function of the list, there can be no doubt that it contained the names of Skirving's Scottish political contacts. Neither Kidston nor Lawson appear to have attended any of the radicals' conventions, but Hislop, 'The Reverend Democrat', was delegated by his local Shotts society to the first convention.[26] In Stirling, which had a large Burgher population and, in 1792, a thriving society of the Friends of the People, it was reported that the 'daemon' of 'political jealousy' had its origins in 'dissentient principles in religion',[27] while in Perth several of the seceding clergy, including most notably the assistant Burgher minister, Jedidiah Aikman (1751-1833), had taken a prominent part in the reform movement.[28]

Of these Burgher ministers the most interesting is George Lawson, if for no other reason than that his views on the political issues of the 1790s are known in more detail than those of his colleagues. Lawson's hostility to the conservatism of his day is clear. Writing at the height of the loyalist reaction in 1793, during 'the stormy days of Muir and Palmer', he attacked conservatism's persecuting spirit, urged forbearance and toleration in political debate, and argued passionately and bravely in support of the freedom of speech and of the press. He declared that

> We ought to cultivate friendship with our neighbours who differ from us in political views. ... What title have you to assume the province of the great Judge who searcheth the hearts and trieth the reins of the children of men? Consider the effect that different educations, and different turns of mind, and different sets of acquaintance, and different capacities and degrees of attention, and better or worse means of information, have in diversifying men's judgment on the same subject. ... Perhaps you are an enemy to all those meetings which have assembled to deliberate on an application to Parliament for a redress of public grievances. Enjoy your own opinion. Act in pursuance of it. But violate not the charity you owe to your neighbours who differ from you. Accuse them not of seditious principles without proof.[29]

This was something more than a worthy appeal for Christian charity in political debate: it was a direct and unequivocal attack upon both the Loyalist Associations and the government for attempting to criminalise their opponents. It is not certain whether Lawson ever became a member of the Society of the Friends of the People, but his sympathy for their cause is clear. Writing during the dark days of 1793, he stated that 'We ought to concur in every regular and seasonable attempt to improve the advantages, and to obtain redress of the grievances of our country',[30] and, when an indiscreet political conversation in the even darker days of 1794 led to his being reported to the Sheriff of Selkirkshire, he wrote to the Sheriff's wife stating that he was fully convinced of the constitutionalism of the radical reformers' proceedings and objectives and that he 'favoured their views'.[31]

Lawson's views were, as we shall see, remarkably similar to those of Archibald Bruce (1746-1816), the Antiburgher Professor of Divinity and minister of Whitburn, who is best remembered, if he is remembered at all, for the rigid theological conservatism which led him to oppose all attempts from 1796 onwards to remodel the Antiburghers' testimony in accordance with 'new light' principles and eventually to withdraw from the Synod and form, with a small group of supporters including Thomas McCrie, the Constitutional Presbytery in 1806. Bruce, however, deserves to be remembered for something more than his role in establishing the Auld Licht Antiburgher church. He was a vigorous pamphleteer whose works deserve attention because they help to explain why many seceders were attracted into the radical reform movement and why conservatives believed that virtually all seceders were tainted with 'Jacobinism'.

The views expressed in Bruce's early works, *The Kirkiad* (1774) and *The Catechism Modernised* (1791), echoed those of such giants of eighteenth-century Scottish ecclesiastical controversy as Ebenezer Erskine (1680-1754), the father of the Secession, and John Witherspoon (1724-1794), the parish minister of Gifford and a leading figure within the Popular Party before his appointment as President of the College of New Jersey at Princeton. In *The Catechism Modernised*, the work which established his reputation, Bruce satirised the doctrinal hypocrisy of a church which kept the Westminster Standards as its official statement of faith and yet preached 'heathenish morality' from its pulpits.[32] Tongue in cheek he offered, in a style strikingly reminiscent of Witherspoon's *Ecclesiastical Characteristics* (1753), to help the Church of Scotland out of its embarrassment by producing new doctrinal standards in the form of a modernised catechism which would be 'more intelligible to modern scholars, more grateful to prevailing taste, and more consonant to present sentiments and practice'.[33] The new standards, he suggested, would be 'infinately more wholesome, genteel and palatable, than the nauseous stuff to be found in such condemned books as the Marrow of Modern Divinity',[34] and would, if accepted, enable the 'beautifying' of the ecclesiastical constitution to proceed apace 'that it may at length grow to a finished and magnificent temple, sacred to the lay patron, the lord of it'.[35] Lay patronage, Bruce claimed, tended to produce a church whose views reflected those of the patrons and, it was implied, were at variance with those of the common people. In effect, it had created an heretical church which served the ungodly interests of the crown (which held the patronage of approximately one third of the parochial presentations in Scotland) and the landowners, and ignored the rights of the poor.

Question: How doth he [i.e. the patron] create a minister?
Answer: He creates the something so called... after his own image, as nearly resembling him in learning, taste, opinions and morals as possible, with absolute dominion over the Christian laity.[36]

The patronage question lay at the heart of the conflict between popular Calvinism and Moderatism in eighteenth-century Scotland. The conflict was about much else as well, as the quotations above from *The Catechism Modernised* illustrate, but patronage was the cause célébre on which it focused. Indeed, patronage disputes, as Robert Small demonstrated, lay behind virtually every individual secession from the Church of Scotland.[37] The patronage issue was certainly theological, but its wider socio-political ramifications were rarely lost sight of during the great debate which raged on through much of the eighteenth century. In 1782 one pamphleteer declared that 'The law of patronage so far from being salutary, can subserve no purpose but to increase the power of an aristocracy already too powerful, and to add to that system of corruption become already far too prevalent'.[38] Twelve years later, Archibald Bruce echoed these sentiments, declaring that

> Both in the first and second reformations of Scotland [1560 and 1638-43], a number of the nobility there acquired great fame and power, by zealously espousing the cause of popular liberty and reformation, in opposition to the tyranny of the crown and church united. But this honourable cause they have long since deserted: they have conspired with the court party in England, and the despotic clergy of Scotland [i.e. the Moderates] to oppress the Presbyterian Church, by the rigorous exercise of ecclesiastical patronage, to the total abolition of the constitutional right of free elections. The burden of the struggle for liberty and reform, against all those powerful interests combined, is now wholly devolved on the inferior and poorer sort of the people, with whom the former or higher class have now completely lost their credit and influence. Knowing that they have in a great manner transferred their attentions, their patriotism, their hopes and their affection to England, the Commons of Scotland can no longer honour their peers with confidence, nor do they give themselves great concern about anything relating to them.[39]

Such opinions were likely to draw those holding them into supporting the sort of radical political reforms which would take power away from the hated nobility and place it in the hands of the common people, and by 1794 Bruce was publicly espousing the cause of the Friends of the People. In that year he published, under the pseudonym of 'A North British Protestant', a pamphlet entitled *Reflections on Freedom of Writing* in which he joined Lawson of the Burgher Synod in defending the liberty of the press, criticising the repressive measures of Pitt's administration, and voicing support for the parliamentary reform movement. He warned that in 'the maxims disseminated and measures lately recommended by the present administration ... the germ of religious intolerance and of persecution for conscience sake may be seen ready to bud and spring up from the same root which has already emitted the luxuriant stalk of political intolerance',[40] and declared that he was 'glad to see so many spirited advocates raised up to plead the cause of political freedom and the right of prosecuting a civil reform'.[41] He was careful to deny that the church in its corporate capacity had any interest in promoting a reform of the civil constitution, but decided in his support for the proposition that Christians had a duty to promote such reforms when they were required for the good of society. That the Christian people of Britain were called to such a duty, he hinted strongly, was clear:

> If it be true, as has often been asserted, and never disproved, that in Britain corruption, in various branches, has grown to such a scandalous height, as to outrage all morality and common honesty, as well as religion;—if places of public trust are openly bought and sold, if the representatives of a nation are rendered mercenary and servile by bribery and undue influence, if oaths and perjuries are nothing accounted of, if profusion, drunkenness, riot, and intrigue are the chief marks of the times for public elections ... if many enormities like these prevail, why should any man be condemned for giving his voice or quota of assistance for providing a remedy.[42]

Archibald Bruce's political opinions were grounded in what might be termed his libertarian-presbyterian interpretation of British history. In his *Historico-Politico-Ecclesiastical Dissertation*, which appeared in 1802, Bruce argued that, whereas the reformation in England had been an act of state, in Scotland it had been the product of a popular revolt. The consequence, he maintained, was that, while the English reformation had not been accompanied by any increase in civil liberty and had seen the royal prerogative augmented, in Scotland the reformation 'had produced a very remarkable struggle for civil rights and popular liberty, which ... eventually procured a system of national rights and legal privileges, civil and religious, which many of their neighbours have anxiously sought, but have not yet attained'.[43] The rights and privileges won at the time of the covenanting revolution had subsequently been lost, but, like the heroes of the later covenanters 'from the eminent Guthrie down to Renwick [who] are accounted martyrs for liberty as well as religion',[44] Bruce and his friends were determined to persevere in the struggle to regain their civil and religious liberties. It was fruitless, Bruce argued, to seek one and ignore the other, for both were inextricably linked. The old covenanter put the matter plainly in his *Reflections on Freedom of Writing*, explaining that

> Civil and religious liberty are but two great branches of the same expanded tree. They have ever been found most intimately allied. They have both had the same common enemies; and nearly the same pretexts and methods have been employed to undermine and destroy both. ... These considerations should inspire the friends of civil and religious liberty, and the promoters of political and ecclesiastical reform, with unanimity.[45]

There was a clear need for all the friends of civil and religious liberty to unite in opposition to a government whose measures were apparently modelled on those of the hated House of Stewart. In his *Historico-Politico-Ecclesiastical Dissertation* Bruce drew an explicit analogy between the Black Acts of 1584 and 'others of a similar spirit in Charles II's time' and the proceedings of 'cabinet ministers and crown lawyers' in prosecuting those 'who promoted popular meetings for presenting petitions and grievances to the legislature, during the late political fever'.[46] Elsewhere he warned that 'A Popish and

Jacobitish faction, and men of high, prelatical, and persecuting principles have not ceased hitherto in Britain to disturb its peace, and threaten its liberty and reformation, and it is to be feared that, under a pretext of loyalty to the king and zeal for the present government, they have of late obtained by degrees to too great credit and power'.[47] The historical analogy was completed by the suggestion that in opposing the despotic measures of Pitt's administration the political reformers of Bruce's own time had inherited the mantle of the covenanters. 'The changes brought about in favour of religion and liberty in the reign of Charles I and afterwards', Bruce wrote, 'though begun and carried on by petitions, remonstrances, popular meetings, conventions of delegates and tables, renovation of covenants and solemn leagues, long disallowed by royal authority and generally stigmatised by papists, despotic prelates, and malignants, as tumults, sedition, and rebellion, are considered now as a glorious reformation'.[48]

It is very tempting to assume that those seceders who supported the Scottish Friends of the People did so for reasons similar to those put forward by Archibald Bruce. Some evidence can be adduced in support of this theoretically attractive assumption. For example, William Skirving, the Burgher seceder who served as secretary to the Scottish Friends of the People, argued at the British Convention that the members of both the convention and 'the primary societies should subscribe a solemn league and covenant' binding them to support the dangerously confrontationalist policies adopted by the convention,[49] and compared, at his trial for sedition in January 1794, the authorities' repressive measures against the reformers with those taken against the covenanters during the Restoration period.[50] Equally suggestive is the intriguing memorial drawn up for the information of the French Directory by Thomas Muir upon his arrival in Paris in December 1797, in which the former leading light of the Scottish Friends of the People outlined his own version of modern Scottish political history. Muir explained how, when James VI acceded to the English throne and attempted to destroy the liberties of the Scottish people, the presbyterian party, which had 'always turned tyrants pale and sometimes hurled them from the throne to the scaffold', rose up to resist Stewart despotism. He estimated that 70,000 presbyterian 'republicans' had been killed in the resultant struggle, and bitterly attacked those historians in the pay of the English court who had portrayed the noble efforts of the covenanters to secure their country's independence and liberty as nothing more than the furious expression of fanaticism.[51] What is especially interesting about this memorial is that it was drawn up not by a seceder but by a former elder of Cadder parish church who had attended the General Assembly of the Church of Scotland. It would seem that the covenanting tradition in Scottish politics attracted devotees even from within a church which had long since abandoned its support for the Covenants themselves.

It might be expected that the strength of the covenanting tradition in late eighteenth-century Scottish popular politics would be reflected in the publications of the societies of the Friends of the People. An examination of these works, however, reveals references to and quotations from Whig writers like Locke and Blackstone, and from philosophes such as Montesquieu, rather than appeals to the authority of covenanting propagandists. This omission does not appear to have been owing to the lack of space available to develop arguments in newspaper advertisements and handbills, for there is nothing of a covenanting hue to be found in the pamphlets which were published in 1792 to argue the case for radical parliamentary reform. Indeed, it is striking that one such pamphlet, George Lawson's *Thoughts on Liberty*, which echoes Archibald Bruce's millennarian views on the French Revolution and his democratic Calvinist critique of Paine's *Rights of Man*, should buttress its arguments with quotations from Montesquieu rather than, say, Alexander Shields.[52]

This refusal to appeal to the covenanting tradition was, in part, at least, founded upon the perceived need to avoid sectarian divisions within a movement which sought to build what would now be termed 'a popular front'. In religious terms, the Scottish democratic movement of the 1790s was an alliance between Calvinism and rationalism. For example, it was reported in February 1793 that in Montrose the Reverend Frederick 'McFarlane's society keeps very frequent meetings in the same house which William Christie kept for a preaching place'.[53] The situation in Montrose, where Antiburgher and Unitarian worked hand-in-hand for the same political goal, represented in extreme form what was happening across Scotland in the early 1790s. This improbable alliance naturally produced tensions. When, on 22 November 1793, Andrew Newton moved that the British Convention appoint a General Fast and Day of Humiliation, he stirred up a hornet's nest. His motion, while it was strongly supported by a number of delegates including George Mealmaker who delivered a long speech in the style of a 'Tent Sermon', was proposed 'amidst laughter',[54] and provoked opposition not only from those who argued that it tended 'to render the convention ridiculous, by enacting what they neither had right to enact nor power to enforce' but also from those who argued that it tended 'to blend religion with politics [and] to divide the friends of reform'.[55] The next day, James Gartley and William Ross, in an attempt to prevent such scenes recurring, proposed that the convention should not receive 'any motion that may tend to a religious discussion',[56] and this motion was only withdrawn when it was pointed out that as 'the convention might reject any motion proposed, they could avoid religious discussions by throwing out such motions as might have that tendency'.[57] By 1794, however, the Edinburgh radicals had decided to make it one of the 'Fundamental Principles or Regulations of the Society' that 'No member shall introduce religious topics into debate, nor motion for prayers to be said, either at the beginning or dismission of the societies, because everything that tends to strife and diversion must be avoided'.[58]

There was, however, almost certainly another reason behind the Scottish Friends of the People's wariness of the covenanting tradition. A movement which sought to avoid confrontation with government by channelling discontent along constitutional lines and presenting its case for parliamentary reform in impeccably moderate language, was not likely to want to undermine its efforts by appealing to the example of men who had rebelled against their king and established a revolutionary government. It was only in 1794, with the movement's organisation virtually destroyed and its leadership en route to exile in Botany Bay, that some groups of radicals decided upon a revolutionary strategy and, in one case at least, sought to justify their rebellion with a declaration more reminiscent of the Sanquhar Declaration of 1680 than Paine's *Rights of Man*. It was a group of Lanarkshire weavers who posted up handbills and circulated letters to possible allies in the west of Scotland declaring that

> In the Name of God We do cast of the Authority of that Tyrant and Usurper known by the name of George III Rex for his Treachyry & perjury in violating the whole laws of both God & man usurping the Hidship of the Church, introducing Popery and slavery, imposing enormous Taxes, Squandering the public revenues, overawing the Parliaments by filling it [sic] up with his Creatures, oppressing the people of Britain and Ireland with packed Courts, vagabond Lawers, Gadgers, half-pay Officers, Liqwise carrying on an unjust and unlawful war, contrary to the minds of the people, and stoping all redress of Grivance in confining any who offer to speak their Sentiments on the times; for these and many more reasons, We declare War against him by taking up Arms & standing one by another to the utmost of our power.[59]

NOTES

1. This paper was first presented in draft form at the Association of Scottish Historical Studies symposium on 'Dissent, Protest and Rebellion in Pre-Industrial Scotland', held at the University of St Andrews, October 1987.
2. W.L. Mathieson, *Church and Reform in Scotland. A history from 1797 to 1843* (Glasgow, 1916), 115; J. Mitchell, 'Memories of Ayrshire', *Scottish History Society*, 3rd Series, XXXIII (1939), 280-1. Mitchell, the son of an Antiburgher minister, was born in 1768 in the village of Beith where he stayed until 'he went to College about the age of fifteen'. *Ibid.*, 245, 255.
3. Mons. B-de, *Reflections on the Causes and Probable Consequences of the Late Revolution in France; with a view of the Ecclesiastical and Civil Constitution of Scotland, and of the progress of its Agriculture and Commerce* (Dublin, 1790), 82-4.
4. *The Scots Magazine*, LXIII (1801), 389-91.
5. G. Robertson, *Rural Recollections; or, the progress of Improvement in Agriculture and Rural Affairs* (Irvine, 1829), 98-100.
6. J. McKerrow, *History of the Secession Church* (Edinburgh, 1839), Vol I, 105.
7. *Ibid.*, 84.
8. *Ibid.*, 238-9, 247-9.
9. In 1798 Lord Advocate Dundas estimated that 'the great Body of the Seceders of this Country' numbered 'near 100,000 Persons', but he seems to have been referring only to the Burghers. In a later letter, the same writer estimated that the total number of seceders amounted to 150,000 in 1795. Robert Dundas, Edinburgh, to Henry Dundas, 1 May 1798. NLS. Melville Papers, MS7, f.196. Robert Dundas, Arniston, to Robert Saunders Dundas, 14 November 1807. NLS. Melville Papers, MS8, ff.203-6.
10. Robert Dundas, Arniston, to Henry Dundas, 10 October 1794. NLS. Melville Papers, MS6, f.193.
11. Sir William Murray, Ochtertyre, to the Duke of Atholl, 7 July 1794. Atholl Muniments, Blair Castle. 59(1)255.
12. Robert Dundas, Arniston, to Robert Saunders Dundas, 14 November 1807. *Loc.cit.*
13. See J. Young, *Essays on the Following Interesting Subjects: viz. I. Government. II. Revolutions. III. The British Constitution. IV. Kingly Government. V. Parliamentary Representation and Reform. VI. Liberty and Equality. VII. Taxation and VIII. The Present War, and the Stagnation of Credit as Connected with it* (Edinburgh, 1794); A. Shanks, *Peace and Order Recommended to Society, in an Address to the Associate Congregation of Jedburgh, from Jeremiah XXIX, 7* (Edinburgh, 1793).
14. Robert Dundas, Arniston, to Robert Saunders Dundas, 14 November 1807. *Loc.cit.*
15. William Porteous, Glasgow, to Robert Dundas, 2 October 1794. NLS. Melville Papers, MS6, ff.197-8.
16. SRO. Minutes of the General Associate Synod. CH3/144/3, p.23.
17. It was not until 5 May 1802 that the Synod 'agreed ... to expunge their minute of 5 May 1795 respecting Mr Young', *Ibid.*, 216.
18. William Porteous, Glasgow, to Robert Dundas, 2 October 1794. *Loc.cit.*
19. Anonymous information on the Perth Friends of the People, n.d. SRO. Home Office Correspondence (Scotland). RH2/4/64, f.341.
20. Spy's reports on the proceedings of the first convention of the Scottish Friends of the People. SRO. Home Office Correspondence (Scotland). RH2/4/66, f.342.
21. J.B. [a government spy], Edinburgh, to William Scott, 30 April 1793. SRO. Home Office Correspondence (Scotland). RH2/4/70, ff.186-90.

22. T.J. Howell, *A Complete Collection of State Trials and Proceedings for High Treason and other Crimes and Misdemeanours from the Earliest Period to the Year 1783, with notes and other illustrations: compiled by T.B. Howell, Esq., F.R.S., F.S.A., and continued from the Year 1783 to the Present Time: by Thomas Jones Howell, Esq. [State Trials]*, XXIV (London, 1818), 564.

23. Declaration of George Mealmaker, 18 June 1794. SRO. Home Office Correspondence (Scotland). RH2/4/76, f.130.

24. List of Persons, n.d. SRO. Justiciary Records. Small Papers. Main Series. JC26/280.

25. P. Mackenzie, *The Trial of William Skirving, with an original memoir and notes* (Glasgow, 1836), 3.

26. Spy's reports on the proceedings of the first convention of the Scottish Friends of the People. SRO. Home Office Correspondence (Scotland). RH2/4/66. f.343.

27. *The Statistical Account of Scotland. Drawn up from the Communications of the Ministers of the Different Parishes*, VIII (Edinburgh, 1793), 295.

28. G. Penny, *Traditions of Perth, containing sketches of the manners and customs of the inhabitants and notices of public occurrences, during the last century* (Perth, 1836), 70, 174.

29. J. Macfarlane, *The Life and Times of George Lawson, D.D., Selkirk, Professor of Theology to the Associate Synod. With glimpses of Scottish character from 1720 to 1820* (Edinburgh, 1862), 393-4.

30. *Ibid.*, 396.

31. *Ibid.*, 384-5. He added, however, that he thought meetings to promote the cause of reform 'would at this time [i.e. following the revolutionary 'Pike Plot' scare of May 1794] be very unseasonable'.

32. A. Bruce, *The Catechism Modernised: and adapted to the meridian of patronage and late improvements in the Church of Scotland: with suitable creeds and prayers* (n.p., 1791), III-IV.

33. *Ibid.*, V.

34. *Ibid.*, VI.

35. *Ibid.*, VII.

36. *Ibid.*, II.

37. R. Small, *History of the Congregations of the United Presbyterian Church from 1733 to 1900* (Edinburgh, 1904), *passim*.

38. Anon., *An Address to the People of Scotland, on Ecclesiastical and Civil Liberty* (Edinburgh, 1782), 15.

39. A. Bruce, *Reflections on Freedom of Writing, and the Impropriety of Attempting to Suppress it by Penal Laws. Occasioned by a Late Proclamation against Seditious Publications, and the Measures Consequent upon it; Viewed Chiefly in the Aspect they Bear to Religious Liberty and Ecclesiastical Reform* (n.p., 1794), 88.

40. *Ibid.*, IV-V.

41. *Ibid.*, V.

42. A. Bruce, *A Brief Statement and Declaration of the Genuine Principles of Seceders, respecting Civil Government, the Duty of Subjects, and National Reformation: and a Vindication of their conduct in reference to some late plans and societies of political reform, and the public dissentions of the time* (n.p., 1799), 51.

43. A. Bruce, *A Historico-Politico-Ecclesiastical Dissertation on the Supremacy of Civil Powers in Matters of Religion; Particularly the Ecclesiastical Supremacy Annexed to the English Crown* (Edinburgh, 1802), 86-7.

44. A. Bruce, *A Serious View of the Remarkable Providences of the Times; and a warning as to the Public Sins, Dangers, and Duty of British Protestants. First read to an Associate congregation in Scotland at the beginning of the French War; now published*

with an introduction relating to the present alarming state of Great Britain (Glasgow, 1795), 81.
45. A. Bruce, *Reflections on Freedom of Writing*, III.
46. A. Bruce, *A Historico-Politico-Ecclesiastical Dissertation*, 94.
47. A. Bruce, *A Serious View of the Remarkable Providences of the Times*, 42.
48. *Ibid.*, 79.
49. T.J. Howell, *State Trials*, XXIII (London, 1817), 438.
50. *Ibid.*, 497.
51. Memorial of Thomas Muir, endorsed '1797 Ecosse'. Ministère des Relations Extérieures, Archives Diplomatiques, Paris. Mémoires et Documents. Vol 1, ff.153-5.
52. D. Lawson, *Thoughts on Liberty, and on Mr Paine's Writings. In a Letter to a Friend* (Paisley, 1792), 6-8, 12-14, 17.
53. Mrs Susan Bean, Montrose, to [H. Dundas?], 24 February 1793. SRO. Home Office Correspondence (Scotland). RH2/4/69, ff.351-8.
54. J.B., Edinburgh, to William Scott, 22 November 1793. SRO. Home Office Correspondence (Scotland). RH/2/4/73, ff220-5.
55. T.J. Howell, *State Trials*, XXIII (London, 1817), 425.
56. *Ibid.*, 428.
57. *Ibid.*, 453.
58. *Ibid.*, 1,304.
59. Copy of letter sent to William Wilson, wright in Strathaven, 22 November 1794. SRO. Melville Muniments. GD51/1/858/2.

4 THE SCOTTISH CONTEXT OF CHARTISM

W. Hamish Fraser

The central question about Scottish chartism is: why did it take the form that it did? Why was it so firmly committed to a moderate, moral force approach? Why were there not more intense demands for change? This, in turn, leads on to questions of class: how far was Chartism a movement of the working class? And this, in its turn, takes us back to the question: how far was a working-class 'made' in Scotland by the 1830s? E.P. Thompson's classic work, *The Making of the English Working Class*, cannot be ignored and Scotland still awaits a similar account. To what extent had the experiences of industrial change and all the accompanying social, political and psychological changes created a working class in which 'some men ... feel and articulate the identity of their interests between themselves, and as against others whose interests are different from them and usually opposed to theirs'?[1]

There is, of course, no easy answer to these questions. One can quickly become immersed in controversial definitions of class, and in unproductive debates over class consciousness and false consciousness, and on the issue of who or what is the authentic voice of the working class. Nonetheless, one has to pursue the question of how far workers had developed 'an identity of interests as between themselves and as against their rulers and employers'.

If trade unionism is a factor in creating class and a measure of its existence, indicating a sense of community of interest by wage earners against their employers,[2] then it developed in the eighteenth century and on into the nineteenth. There has been a tendency to look for the beginnings of an organised labour movement in the textile industry of the late eighteenth and early nineteenth centuries and to paint a picture of a rather docile people in the eighteenth century, accepting with little protest many of the changes that were taking place. That view has recently come under challenge, since it is so obviously out of line with the findings of work that has been done on France by scholars such as William Reddy, Joan Scott and Bill Sewell, all of whom have shown the extent of formal organisations among journeymen artisans. Sewell's work, in particular, has brought out the continuity of language and assumptions that persisted from the eighteenth century well into the nineteenth, arguing that 'The nineteenth century labour movement was born in the craft workshops, not in the dark satanic mills'. Such work has influenced British historians like John Rule and I.J. Prothero, both of whom have effectively rescued the experience of the English artisan. It would be surprising if Scotland were different and my own recent work shows that this was not so.[3]

Groups of artisans were organising from at least the 1720s: most notably of all, the journeymen tailors in Edinburgh who had an effective and, more or less, continuous organisation from the 1720s until the 1820s. They and other groups made constant use of strikes, petitions and appeals to the courts to try to improve hours, wages and general conditions. Organisation emerged in response to the transformation of economy and society that took place in the eighteenth century. There were great variations in the pattern of response, as each trade developed its own tactics and timing. The moment of change and the circumstances of change were never exactly the same in each trade and transformation did not follow some single clearly-defined track. Undoubtedly, however, one group of tradesmen learned from another.

The first journeymen organisations had been mutual aid societies, providing assistance at times of sickness and unemployment and to widows and orphans, through charitable boxes. When the need arose, these bodies could be readily transformed into industrial associations. By the middle of the eighteenth century the increasing number of occasions on which this was happening reflected the whole series of changes that was taking place within crafts. The trade incorporations were losing their regulatory control over crafts; the units of productions were getting larger. With more and bigger workshops, the social distance between employer and journeyman was getting wider. It was rarer for apprentices actually to live in a master's house and a formally paternalist relationship was being replaced by, essentially, a cash one. Customary patterns of wages, recruitment and discipline were giving way to more varied and more erratic ones. The result was more frequent opportunities for conflict.

Initially, skilled men were at an advantage, since their skills were at a premium and in many sectors of industry employers were desperate to attract wherever they could and paid wages above the norm to achieve this. It gave journeymen opportunities to press for higher wages and improved work patterns and they frequently did so. Their organisations were not ephemeral bodies, but had a continuous existence over a number of years. Even if they disappear from public view for a few years, it is apparent that, when the need for mutual action arose, journeymen in most crafts knew who the potential leaders were and how to bring the organisation back into effective life. There was nothing in the Scottish law to discourage such activities. Combination of workmen was not illegal in Scotland, since the law allowed workers to combine to ask the trade incorporation or the town council for a change in work conditions. If that failed they had the right of recourse to the courts of law. It was an offence to coerce employers by strike action and journeymen leaders did land in prison, but, both local magistrates and the judges of the Court of Session showed a readiness to lend an ear to the complaints of workers. This is less remarkable than it might at first seem when one remembers that the prime concern of the Scottish landed classes—and, of course, in the late eighteenth century, the lawyers and judges of Edinburgh were to all intents an adjunct of that class—was the maintenance of social order.

They were, therefore, ready to interfere in industrial relations if that were the means of maintaining social peace. With increased political and social tensions in the last decade of the century they were even more ready to do so and viewed the tensions created by unregulated industrial relations as a threat to social stability. At the same time as Braxfield and his associates were despatching the radicals Muir, Gerald, Margarot, Palmer and so on to Botany Bay, other judges and justices were using their right of intervention to try to maintain some kind of just wage, which bore some relationship to the cost of living, and making use of comparisons with England and between trades.

There were, however, conflicting pressures. Intellectual arguments that barriers to the exercise of market forces had to be removed were gaining ground. Fears of the increased insubordination of the poor led many to see journeymen's organisations as a threat, and to call for restriction. In law, as in language, there was a growing tendency to argue for assimilation with the English pattern. The first decade of the nineteenth century brought a debate in legal circles that increasingly swung against interventionism.

The greatest pressures for change came from within the expanding manufacturing sector of the west. They came to a head in 1812 with the Scottish weavers' strike which followed the successful appeal to the courts by the Lanarkshire weavers for regulation of wage rates. Wage-fixing legislation was swept away. Handloom weavers found their earnings sliding rapidly. But other groups too were coming under pressure. The old scarcity of labour was giving way to labour surpluses. There was an acceleration of the movement off the land into the city, with a rapid deterioration in urban living conditions. Workers' mutual aid societies were collapsing under pressure of demand. At the same time, clergy, heritors and the urban middle class were adopting harder attitudes towards the distribution of poor relief. For many, the second decade of the century brought a massive deterioration in conditions. Little wonder hopes began to be pinned on a millennialist rescue from distress through political action and even on direct insurrectionary action. That dream ended with the repression that followed the 'Radical Rising' of 1820.

The deterioration in the position of other groups of workers was rather more subtle than in the West of Scotland, but none the less real. The pace of change quickened after 1815 as new employers came in and pressure for increased output grew.

As the economy moved out of depression in 1820, a rapid expansion took place in many traditional crafts. In Edinburgh, for example, demand for tailors reached a spectacular peak in 1822, when the visit of George IV to the city brought in the Scottish gentry in their thousands.[4] All those kilts, plaids, hats, dresses and military uniforms required every available tailor. The wages of many of them doubled or more. But, it also pulled in the less than skilled and, with the excitement passed, the pressure on wages and trends towards reorganisation of the trade returned. After a century the Edinburgh journeymen tailors' society collapsed as ready-made clothing, much made by sweated labour at home came in.

Equally devastating was the experience of the building workers. For three years, 1822-24, there was an unrestrained speculative boom in the building of Edinburgh's New Town. At its height some 3,000 masons alone were finding work. Wages rose from 18s to 24s per week; those of the joiners from 15s to 25s, of plasterers, who were especially scarce, from 16s to 28s. Clearly, scarcity brought gains. But, it also had long-lasting, adverse implications. There was much more use of subcontracting by builders, hiring building gangs, rather than employing tradesmen directly. With country workers arriving in vast numbers, it was no great problem to establish the new system. Once established it was hardly possible to eradicate it. With the collapse of the boom in the summer of 1825, as credit dried up, thousands of building workers were thrown idle. By the end of 1827 there were fewer than 100 masons left in Edinburgh. The building industry stagnated for a decade and in all trades linked to it gains made over previous decades were lost.

Yet another group, the book trades, lost ground in the aftermath of the collapse of Constables and Ballantynes. The great boom in publishing sustained by Sir Walter Scott's novels, the *Encyclopaedia Britannica* and the political and literary reviews, which began to flourish in the early nineteenth century, had pulled the poorly qualified into the trade. More and more apprentices were taken on. When the collapse came that older cohesion which allowed organisations to survive bad times had been destroyed. It was long before workers in the book trades regained effective bargaining powers.

By the early nineteenth century, there had been an artisan-based, organised working class, effectively united in trade societies. These from time to time, and with increasing regularity, were collaborating during disputes, giving mutual support across trade boundaries, operating joint committees to petition Parliament—all very much on the pattern described by E.P. Thompson. By the 1820s this was at least badly undermined, if not destroyed. Unions collapsed, status and earnings plummetted. Of course, craft unions reappeared and re-organised in the 1830s, with attempts to form federal national unions. But the old pattern had been effectively smashed—at any rate in the cities. It is probable that more of it survived in the small towns, because they always had the safety valve of migration to the cities. Not surprisingly, chartism, which had an appeal to the artisan tradition, was strongest in the small towns. Other groups too went down to defeat in the 1820s. Miners and cotton spinners both fought prolonged battles, essentially over trying to maintain some kind of craft-like control over their work processes. Who should be employed? Who should dictate the speed and pattern of work—the worker or the employer? Both groups lost out. The spinners' union at least survived: the miners did not effectively re-organise until the 1840s.

By the early 1830s, then, far from there being the 'making of the Scottish working class', one had (to use a phrase of Chris Whatley's) 'the breaking of the working class'. Few trades were able to maintain control of entry or restrictions on apprenticeship. Rapid urbanisation—faster, after all, than in most other parts of Britain—brought the unskilled and the half-skilled into the trades. True there were attempts at re-organising and re-grouping, schemes for general unions were there. But, in fact, trade unions were probably speaking for a smaller proportion of the working population than in the 1820s.

The final breaking-up came with the cotton spinners' strike in 1837,[5] when the full weight of united capitalism, plus the state, was brought to bear to smash the hand mulespinners' union. It was the end of an era. The union did not disappear—nor did the spinners entirely lose their autonomy in the workplace—but it never regained the significant, vanguard role it had achieved in the 1820s and 1830s. Like the miners' strike of 1984-85, the implications of the defeat of the spinners went far beyond their own union. It had great symbolic importance, marking the defeat and break-up of an organisation that, for two decades, had been the most tightly-knit and dynamic in Scottish society. It was a deterrent to vigorous action. Trade-union leaders could be held criminally responsible for the action of their members. Thanks to the publicity efforts of Sheriff Alison, unions in Scotland were branded as violent, murderous and drunken. There are signs that workers were dissociating themselves from the unions. The depression of the next five years allowed employers to consolidate the assault on trade-union control. It was the completion of the process begun in the 1820s. There was now a substantial reserve of labour. Highland clearances, rural change and Irish immigration provided employers with a ready pool of relatively cheap labour.

Dorothy Thompson, the foremost authority on the subject, has no doubt about the importance of the cotton spinners' case as a crucial precipitant of chartism.[6] It was reported in detail in Feargus O'Connor's *Northern Star*. Feargus himself, Augustus Beaumont and Joseph Rayner Stephens all came up to Scotland and made blood-curdling speeches denouncing the authorities. Dr John Taylor made much of the case throughout the north of England. It was a factor in explaining the (claimed) 200,000 turn out for the first chartist rally in Glasgow in May 1838. In Scotland, however, attitudes were ambivalent. No doubt many were intimidated by the ferocity of the law. Yet others were not entirely warm in their feelings towards the spinners. Like the miners, this was a group slightly apart from the rest of the working class. They were, as Alison said, an aristocracy of labour. They were not a particularly well-loved group. While the arrest and trial of the spinners undoubtedly caused much indignation, there was not that upswell of protest such as the case of the Tolpuddle Martyrs had brought. There were no sympathetic strikes. The chartist leaders tried to make mileage out of it to forge that link they sought between trade unions and chartism; but it never really caught on as a major *cause célèbre* among the Scottish workers. As has been argued, Scottish unions were now effectively weakened, and unemployment was rising, but, also, other unions were wary about being seen to approve of violence, no matter how indirectly. With Daniel O'Connell and others demanding the imposition of harsh combination laws,[7] the weak Scottish unions saw discretion as the better part of valour.

What the cotton spinners' case did was to strengthen traditional radical arguments that the real need was for political change. Only political reform would alter a system where law could be corrupted and where law was monopolised by those who held political power. Scottish workers had tra-

ditionally placed great faith in the law, despite the unpleasant experiences of
the radical period. Generally, they clung to the idea that one could look to
the law for redress. Groups like handloom weavers still believed that it was
not too late for it to be called in to regulate wages. The chartists had some
success in propagating the view that the law had somehow fallen into the
hands of those who were enemies to the workers. Such an analysis, as
Stedman Jones has argued, meant that improvement could come through
changing the political system.[8] Similarly, since it was the *state*, rather than
the employers, which had broken the cotton spinners' union, it seemed that
the need was for political enfranchisement to influence the state.

Of course, this very experience of change, of proletarianisation, could in
itself create a sense of exploitation and alienation which would in turn
contribute to a sense of class, and clearly there are signs of this. There
emerged, in the 1820s, an analysis that blamed economic structures, rather
than excessive taxation or corruption in government, for the plight of the
workers. This was almost inevitable in view of the theories of the political
economists, which were increasingly being preached by every possible
means.[9] The new orthodoxy had been forming for decades, but, in the late
eighteenth and early nineteenth century, it had been challenged again and
again in the courts. In the years of distress and displacement after 1815 there
was a concentrated effort from pamphlet and pulpit to popularise a standard
view. The message was that economic forces operated independently of
human intervention, guided by 'laws', just as in the world of the physical
sciences, which it was impossible and misguided for mortal man to try to
defy. Any restriction on freedom of trade, or of the labour market, by means
of government intervention or of trade-union action was to be abhorred, as a
defiance of such 'fundamental' laws, and any way was bound to be ineffective.
Improvement could come through moral restraint or emigration to reduce
population size, so that the means of subsistence were not overwhelmed. In
response to this, there did gradually emerge a series of views among working-
class radicals that together made up an alternative view. This blamed com-
petitiveness, the very essence of capitalism, for the plight of the workers and
for the deterioration in their position from what was seen, increasingly, as
an earlier golden age. The handloom weavers adopted this view most strongly,
with their faith in the formation of trade boards to maintain a minimum wage.
In the weavers' analysis, the cause of their plight was excessive competition,
brought about by 'adventurers in the trade', who pushed down prices. They
believed that a trade board, consisting of an equal number of masters and
men, would support the rates paid by 'honourable' employers and would
'equalise, superintend and regulate the prices of workmanship'.[10] In this way
'dishonourable' employers, who were using unprincipled competition and
forcing respectable manufacturers to push down prices and, therefore, wages
would be forced out and old harmonies be restored. Here was no class analysis,
but one that identified good employers with workmen. But, it did contribute
to a political analysis. If only the political system could be altered to allow Sir
John Maxwell's bill on trade boards through Parliament then the situation of
the handloom weaver could be righted.

Yet others searched for alternatives: in community, the short-lived Orbiston experiment; in efforts at co-operative production taken up, on paper, at any rate, by many trade unionists; in co-operative trading, pushed by the ubiquitous Alexander Campbell and by the later chartist, William Thomson. There was, however, a constant ambivalence about the objectives of all of these. The complete opting out, setting up a community apart from the world that would lead to the gradual conversion of the world by example—Owenism at its most pure—was not something that attracted many. Much more appealing was the trades' union which would provide some employment to the labour surplus and so ensure that the wages of those employed remained adequate. It was an idea pushed strongly in the Scottish unstamped press in the early 1830s. Essentially the idea was to get people out of the labour market: in a way, of course, an adaptation of classical political economy. A third variation was that through unity, sobriety and the exercise of a little self-denial, workers would become self-employed—their own capitalists and employers. Here was a harking back to the world of the independent artisan, working at his own pace, as his own master. But, of course, it also had echoes of the new orthodoxy, that in the new capitalist society there were opportunities for all to become capitalists. The confusion of looking backward and looking forward is one that persists and is hard to disentangle. It seems to me that from the end of the 1820s there existed side by side and, often in the same people, two conflicting views of change. One was millennialist, one which assumed a transformation of the individual and of society, a sudden recognition of the evil of the present and its replacement by something better, more like what had existed in the past. Alongside that was a view which suggested that through education and personal improvement workers would change and the middle class would recognise the need to treat the poor differently. In collaboration with the middle class a change could be wrought in society. The campaign for an extension of the franchise was part of both processes. One view involved seeking alternatives to industrialism, the other emphasised the possibility of modifying and improving it.

That ambivalence persisted into the chartist period. The millennialist element was there in the chartist churches, the most vital and distinctively Scottish part of the movement. To a large extent, chartist churches appeared in the years between 1839 and 1842 because of the victimisation of chartist families by both the established and the main dissenting churches and by the manifest hostility of the clergy to chartism. And anti-clericalism was the most consistent and persistent feature of Christian chartist sermons. It is a theme that has echoes from earlier periods when the clergy was attacked for their control of poor relief. This was a report of a radical speech of 1819:

> It was asserted that the clergy gulled every government, and that it was their infamous combination with the landed proprietors which had cheated the poor of their rights. All of those who attended church were denounced as hypocrites because they went to hear clergymen descant on charity, morality, and virtues which they well knew the preachers themselves never practised.

It was a sentiment often repeated, in slightly milder tones, in the chartist churches. But Christian chartism was also about creating a community and a fellowship that protected and gave succour against the vicissitudes of life and created a more egalitarian world: 'Christianity is the religion of equality— all men having been created with equal rights are equal before God'.[11] It was about achieving that change of heart that would create a different kind of society. The echoes of Owenism were there in sermons on the theme 'How long shall the wicked triumph?'

One *deus ex machine* that had a similar appeal was total abstinence, pioneered in Scotland from 1828 by John Dunlop in Greenock. The movement originally spoke for moderation in drinking, but by the mid 1830s a total abstinence group had appeared. It was a movement that attracted little support from the middle classes or from the clergy, but it did gain ground among the skilled working class. It too offered a quick way to 'salvation' both in this life and the next. Coupled with education, it was to bring a moral reformation. The *Scottish Patriot*, a short-lived Chartist paper that favoured total abstinence declared that they were 'forming a character for the people which they have never before possessed—making them intelligent by instruction'.[12] It was a campaign that was extraordinarily effective. Scottish voluntary organisations, including trade unions, moved out of pubs as meeting places. By the 1850s it was rare for working-class meetings to be held anywhere where there was drink.

But it was the collaborationist approach that was most utilised in Scotland. Most believed that by convincing the middle classes of working-class improvement and progress middle-class support for working-class advancement could be gained. The period 1833 to 1837 was a period of fairly constant agitation over Ireland and burgh reform, as well as visits of leading political figures like Earl Grey, Lord Durham and Daniel O'Connell to Scotland. As a result, there was a continuous debate among working-class political activists on tactics. Should they join in presentations to such people? Generally, however, the middle-class political activists in Scotland were identified with continuing 'reform' and working-class disillusion was with the failures of Whig Governments, not with the middle class. Fiona Montgomery has taken us through the intricacies of middle-class politics in these years and, what is apparent, is that there were always sections of the middle class who identified with and were able to give leadership, generally restraining leadership, to working-class radicalism.[13] So old reformers, like Turner of Thrushgrove featured at the annual dinners, marking the great Thrushgrove reform meeting of 1816 and linking reformers of all classes. Old radicals like Baillie Craig joined new ones like William Weir. They could all unite in greeting 'Radical Jack' Durham in October 1834 and in getting excited about the threat of a Wellington government at the end of that year. The Glasgow Political Union remained active until 1835, petitioning against the Corn Laws, for the burgh reform bill, removing bishops from the House of Lords, the ballot, the separation of Church and State, against the water bill, for reform of the Lords and so on, all issues that could attract politically-active working-class support.

It is often suggested that in the 1830s 'after the disillusionment of 1832' working-class hostility was largely towards the middle class and that only in the 1840s with the growing success of the Anti-Corn Law league did it turn more to the aristocracy. Fiona Montgomery has questioned this and it is difficult to disagree with her conclusion. It seems that much of the nature of the chartist movement in Scotland can be explained by the fact that the enemy all along was identified as the landed class. There was much less disappointment with 1832 in Scotland than there was in England. After all, it meant a massive increase in the electorate from the few thousand of the unreformed system, and there was no disenfranchisement of workers as happened with the end of 'scot and lot' and 'potwallopers' south of the border.

The traditional identification of 'Old Corruption' as the enemy persisted throughout the period. This is a post-reform paper *The Agitator* in 1833:

> Away with the pageantry of monarchy, and the assumption of aristocracy. Hurl the whole fabric of corruption to the devil along with the rascally crew— the mitred and titled vagabonds who live by usurpation and plunder on public industry... Are we to suffer longer to be taxed, and screwed, and jack-assed, till the very flesh is eaten off our bones, and the blood scotched out of our bodies? It is not this ministry or that ministry that is the cause. It is the system. The cursed hereditary system.

Similarly, there is the *Chartist Circular* of October 1839:

> Hereditary power corrupted the whole government, poisoned the press, demoralised society, prostituted the church, dissipated the resources of the nation, created monopolies, paralysed trade, ruined half the merchants, pro- duced national bankruptcy—it could be overthrown if capitalocracy united with the people.

There was no new poor law in Scotland after 1834 and that removed a major factor which stimulated the agitation that led to Northern chartism in England. Instead, the inadequacies of the Scottish poor law could be blamed on clergy and heritors, not on middle-class ideologues. The religious issues of the 'Ten Year Conflict' again allowed working class and middle class to combine against the landed class. The patronage issue presented as about civil and political rights was anti-landlord. So in both church politics and social politics it was the landed class that was firmly identified as the exploiter, as the cause of distress.

Clearance in the Highlands led to distress, poverty and unemployment in the towns. The arrival of increasing numbers of Irish likewise stemmed from landlord activities in Ireland, support for which led to the corruption of British traditions of liberty by the passing of Coercion Acts. The Irish provided an identifiable scapegoat on whom many ills could be blamed, but here too was a problem created by the landowning class. Significantly, the Scottish bourgeoisie were among the first to see the attractions of the campaign against the Corn Laws. The fact that, despite industrial developments, Scot- land remained overwhelmingly an agricultural society further strengthened this analysis of the nation's ills. The *Scots Times* took up a similar refrain in 1840.

So long as oppressive laws and iniquitous monopolies were maintained by the aristocracy, which equally affected the employer and the employed, it was evident that the competitive system would compel masters to do what in other circumstances they would not think of.

This is a much narrower focus of hostility than was common in England. There was less talk in Scotland of the aristocracy of wealth, of middlemen and factory lords. The parasite element was almost exclusively presented as the landed aristocracy. Despite this, it is somewhat surprising that O'Connor's Land Plan, which envisaged peasant holdings bought by co-operatives or, indeed, Bronterre O'Brien's more ambitious nationalisation ideas received so little response in Scotland. Perhaps it was a measure of how far O'Connor was discredited in Scotland by the 1840s.

One area of potential conflict between middle class and working class was, of course, factory legislation. A reform movement based on powerloom factory weavers had got underway in 1830 when the Glasgow operatives wrote to Peel at the Home Office protesting at fluctuations in employment and at unregulated competition, and calling for state intervention.

We would rather see all parties in moderate employment, with modest remuneration for their labours, than be as we are at present with one party toiling incessantly under the most aggravated circumstances for fifteen hours a day and another strolling the streets in deepest misery.[14]

Only shorter hours would 'restore the operative to the rank which he ought to hold in society'. But, even here, it is apparent that the textile employers did not constitute a homogeneous group and there were divisions between them. Hard men of the Manchester School could not speak for all. Certainly, beyond the ranks of textiles, there were businessmen and their intellectual allies who took a sympathetic view. By the 1840s, there were really no dissident voices against factory reform. The debate was over the technicalities. It did not lead to bitter class confrontation. As Tony Dickson and Tony Clarke's work on Paisley shows, the textile workers there identified the problems of their industry as community ones, not brought on by the employers but by external forces—foreign trade, government policy.[15]

There were other changes in middle-class attitudes that strengthened collaborationst trends. Callum Brown's work has discussed the massive upsurge in evangelical social endeavour, facilitated by the enhanced power and influence that middle-class evangelicals had in local government in the post-war era.[16] Sunday School membership, for example, grew four times as fast as population in Glasgow between 1831 and 1841 and, of course, their schools provided scholars with educational skills. Education was the road to salvation for evangelicals just as much as for many chartists. Literacy was seen as important whether for the Bible or for the political tract. There were efforts also at day education reform, housing reform, sanitary reform under municipal corporation leadership in Glasgow throughout the 1830s and 1840s.

Although most interpretations of chartism see it as a product of and a response to distress or to the social changes accompanying the industrial revolution, as Gareth Stedman Jones has very effectively reminded us, chartism was, first and foremost, a *political* movement and, to quote him,

> political movements cannot satisfactorily be defined in terms of the anger and disgruntlement of disaffected social groups or even the consciousness of a particular class. A political movement is not simply a manifestation of distress and pain, its existence is distinguished by a shared conviction articulating a political solution to distress and a political diagnosis of its causes.[17]

It is doubtful if Scottish chartism ever achieved the necessary cohesiveness for it fully to fit such a definition. To acquire an effective ideology required a systematic and coherent interpretation of the radical past. This seems to be where some of its difficulties arose. Scottish chartism found it very difficult to find an acceptable tradition to draw on. There was a lack of any tradition of lost rights to compare with the 'Norman Yoke' tradition in England, though there were attempts to find inspiration in Wallace and Bruce.[18] The absence of such a tradition created a lack of confidence in calling for universal suffrage. There was no great confidence in democratic procedures. It is always more difficult to demand *new* rights rather than old and one has a constant sense, in reading the chartist press, of the derivative nature of Scottish chartism. The events of 1793, particularly the saintly Joseph Gerald, do feature in chartist literature in terms of the corruption of the law, the injustice of Braxfield, but against this could be set the enlightenment of the Whig lawyers such as Jeffreys and Cockburn. And those despatched to Botany Bay had been middle-class radicals. The way in which this was used to encourage social collaboration was symbolised by the decision to erect a monument to the political martyrs of 1793 on Calton Hill in Edinburgh. Joseph Hume seems to have been the instigator and the reformed Edinburgh Town Council agreed in principle to raising the monument in February 1837. This gave added significance to the Calton Hill resolutions of December 1838 which denounced violence and physical force as a means of achieving political reform. The site was eventually granted in July 1842 and the foundation stone laid by Joseph Hume in November 1844. The families of some of the judges tried to get it stopped, but in May 1847 a very innocuous inscription was agreed that did not denounce the judges by name.

The events of 1820 had almost no place in this interpretation of the past. They were explained as the work of spies and *agents provocateurs*, misleading an, as yet, poorly educated working class. The revelations about Richmond made by Peter MacKenzie in 1831 were intended to show that the political reform movement of 1831-32 was quite different from the radical unrest of 1820. So the studious avoidance of any reference to 1820 by the chartists was part of that same process of emphasising respectability and collaboration.

There was no insurrectionary tradition that was taken up by Scottish radicals. When it appeared briefly in 1848 it was mainly among the Irish, where the tradition was accepted. Indeed, one of the reasons why the resurgence of chartism in 1848 was so muted in Scotland was precisely because it was identified with the Irish who were already present in such numbers as to be perceived as a major threat, and who were already identified as blacklegs and strike breakers. There was little sympathy for the Irish cause. Conversely, the Irish in Scotland had been slow to identify with chartism.

A second reason for the limited nature of the events of 1848 was the shrewdness of the authorities. They had learned lessons from the past. There was a clear determination that there were to be no martyrs—certainly no respectable or middle class ones. Unrest and disturbances in the street were dealt with harshly. The leaders of the 1848 Glasgow food rioters were punished with fifteen years transportation. Sheriff Alison was still a very active Lanarkshire sheriff in the 1840s, harrassing chartist meetings, banning and curbing street demonstrations. On the other hand, nothing was allowed to develop into a *cause célèbre*. The State, in the shape of the law, had learned from the events of 1838 and earlier. On the whole, the Scottish judges handled the Chartist cases with great care. John Saville in his recent book on 1848 paints a contrasting picture for England where, he writes,

> Large parts of the judges' charges to the juries, or their summing up before the juries retired to consider their verdicts, were concerned with instruction on the virtues of English liberty, or the superiority in general of the English system over its European neighbours, or the wickedness, absurdity or illogicality of the political and social doctrines held by the prisoners in the dock.

Shades of 1793. In contrast, in the trial for sedition of John Grant, Henry Ranken and Robert Hamilton in Edinburgh, what was revealed was 'a high-minded and humane judiciary'. The defence counsel, James Moncrieff, commented,

> There have been times when verdicts have been returned under circumstances of public prejudice, in which the voice, not of law merely, but reason and sense, was drowned in one overpowering terror; verdicts which filled some, at least, who pronounced them with undying regret; and have stamped an indelible stigma on the times they characterise. I am under no apprehension of that kind today.[19]

It was a view that most politically aware Scottish working men would probably have accepted in 1848. The institutional and the sociological basis of the reformism which one identifies with the mid century was established during the chartist years. It became more and more difficult for any kind of counter-ideology to be set against the dominant ideology of the middle class. The attack on the millocracy had never developed effectively. Instead, it was criticism of the landed aristocracy that ensured the cheers of the Scottish working class. It ensured the dominance of Liberal politics, often of the most archaic kind, well into the twentieth century. It was an analysis that made it extremely difficult for an independent labour movement to get any effective hold. It too spent its time attacking the aristocracy. Tom Johnston was at his most effective in *Our Scots Noble Families*.[20] Only when that analysis was escaped from, largely because of the break-up of the Liberal Party, could a socialist alternative emerge.

NOTES

1. E.P. Thompson, *The Making of the English Working Class* (1st published, 1963; most recent edn., London, 1980).
2. The Webbs, whose research interests were more concerned with institutions than with class as such, famously remarked that a 'trade union, as we understand the term, is a continuous association of wage-earners for the purpose of maintaining or improving the condition of their working lives'. They found evidence of such associations in England as early as the end of the seventeenth century but not before. S. and B. Webb, *The History of Trade Unionism* (1st published 1894; new edn., London, 1920), 1.
3. e.g. W.M. Reddy, *The Rise of Market Culture: the Textile Trade and French Society 1750-1900* (Cambridge, 1984); Louise A. Tilly and Joan W. Scott, *Women, Work and Family* (London, 1987); William H. Sewell, *Structure and Mobility: the men and women of Marseilles, 1820-1870* (Cambridge, 1985); W.H. Fraser, *Conflict and Class: Scottish Workers 1700-1838* (Edinburgh, 1988).
4. For a recent account of this bizarre, but important, event, see John Prebble, *The King's Jaunt* (Glasgow, 1988); cf. H.R. Trevor-Roper, 'The Invention of Tradition: the Highland Tradition of Scotland', in *The Invention of Tradition*, ed. E. Hobsbawm and T. Ranger (Cambridge, 1983), 15-41, esp. 29-32.
5. For which see W.H. Fraser, 'Glasgow Cotton Spinners, 1837', in *Scottish Themes*, ed. J. Butt and J.T. Ward (Edinburgh, 1978), 80-97.
6. D. Thompson, *The Chartists...* (1984, pbk edn., Aldershot, 1986), 21ff.
7. Daniel O'Connell (1775-1847), known as the 'Liberator' as a result of his fight for Catholic emancipation turned, after the success of that campaign in 1829 to the struggle for the repeal of the Irish Act of Union. To Balzac he 'incarnated a whole people', but in his socio-economic outlook he did not go beyond *laissez-faire* liberalism.
8. See G. Stedman Jones, 'Re-thinking Chartism', in his *Languages of Class: Studies in English Working Class History 1832-1982* (Cambridge, 1983), chapter 3.
9. There is a substantial recent literature on this. For a pioneering article of special relevance to Scotland, see A. Tyrell, 'Political economy, Whiggism and the education of working-class adults in Scotland, 1817-40', *Scottish Historical Review*, XLVIII (1969), 151-65.
10. Parliamentary Papers, 1834, X, *Report of the Select Committee on Handloom Weavers' Petitions*, Q727; *Glasgow Herald*, 19 January 1834. See, on this, M. Berg, *The Machinery Question and the Making of Political Economy* (Cambridge, 1980), esp. 235-49.
11. *Chartist Circular*, 11, 7 December 1839).
12. 'We may not be producing great effects upon the government, but we are forming a character for the people which they never before possessed—making them intelligent by instruction and moral by inculcating the principles of total abstinence ... Universal Suffrage has now been carried from the public arena into the domestic hearth of the working classes. It has become a part of the social character of the people. It is associated with their amusements. It has become identified with their religion'. Quoted from the *Scottish Patriot* of late 1840 or early 1841 by Alexander Wilson, *The Chartist Movement in Scotland* (Manchester, 1970), 124.
13. F.A. Montgomery, 'Glasgow Radicalism 1830-1850' (University of Glasgow Ph.D., 1974); 'Glasgow and the Struggle for Parliamentary Reform, 1830-32', *Scottish Historical Review*, LXI (October 1982), 130-54; and 'The Unstamped Press: the Contribution of Glasgow', *ibid.*, LIX (April, 1980), 154-70.

14. Scottish Record Office, RH 2/4/158, John Stewart and Daniel Macaulay to Sir Robert Peel, 20 February 1830.

15. T. Clarke and T. Dickson, 'Class and Class Consciousness in Early Industrial Capitalism: Paisley 1770-1850', in *Capital and Class in Scotland* ed. Dickson (Edinburgh, 1982), 8-60. The most interesting recent work on factory reform is R. Gray, 'The languages of factory reform in Britain c.1830-1860' in *The Historical Meanings of Work*, ed. Patrick Joyce (Cambridge, 1987), 157-79.

16. Callum Brown, *The Social History of Religion in Scotland* (London, 1987), esp. chapter 5.

17. Stedman Jones, *Language of Class...*, 96.

18. The *locus classicus* for the tradition of the 'Norman Yoke' is Christopher Hill, 'The Norman Yoke', in *Democracy and the Labour Movement* (London, 1954), ed. J. Saville, 11-66.

19. John Saville, *1848: the British State and the Chartist Movement* (Cambridge, 1987), 174-5.

20. T. Johnston, *Our Scots Noble Families* (Glasgow, 1909)—a noted series of articles attacking the landed aristocracy of Scotland first published in Johnston's weekly paper, *Forward*, which broadly supported the Independent Labour Party in Glasgow.

5 CHARTISM IN ABERDEEN: RADICAL POLITICS AND CULTURE 1838-48[1]

Robert Duncan

The 150th anniversary of the launch of the agitation for the People's Charter provides a useful opportunity for beginning a much-needed re-assessment of the chartist and popular radical experience in Scotland. The standard books, by Wright and Wilson[2] are reliable as descriptive and narrative histories, but are deficient in analysis and do not extend to the kind of important questions of theory and interpretation which have increasingly concerned historians of chartism and of labour in the 1970s and 1980s. Such lines of enquiry include, and require, a fuller understanding of class relations and class consciousness; the nature and problems of political mobilisation; contemporary radical perceptions of political strategy and a more sophisticated analysis than the much used and abused simplistic distinction between 'moral force' and 'physical force'; the manifestations and significance of radical and chartist culture, and their relation to opposing and prevailing forms, expressions and controls. The contest for, and exercise of control over the whole gamut of cultural provision—and especially that which was made by and aimed at working people—has recently, and justifiably, gained greater recognition among historians as a vital aspect of class and ideological struggle.[3]

Moreover, if we are conducting a case-study by focusing on particular localities and communities, it is necessary to look for, and grasp an overall picture of social relations, political traditions, and community activism of various shades, including evidence of formal and informal contacts, networks and rivalries among interest groups and individuals, prominent and otherwise. Without that mode of enquiry, there is a danger that the interplay of political and cultural life may be improperly appreciated. It has another implication, in that the complexities of the chartist experience are ill-served by the narrow, institutional 'labour history' approach which has tended to concentrate on the organisational and overtly political sides of working-class movements, separate from the totality of class and social relations in time and place.

It is also mistaken to characterise the chartist movement, merely or predominantly, as a spontaneous reflex of widespread social distress arising out of the episodic trade depressions of the late 1830s and 1840s. Although the high points of the chartist agitations coincided with, and were fuelled by periods of acute economic crises as in 1838-39, 1841-42, and in 1847-48, the rise and decline of chartism as a mass movement was not dictated by, or dependent upon, fluctuations in the trade cycle, as if the latter was a directly responsible barometer of discontent. Rather, the difficulties of chartist mobilisation and morale during the intervening years of apparent economic recovery had little to do with such considerations: they arose, more so, from the pressures of coming to terms with political setbacks and defeats, and the harsh reality of government repression in 1839, 1842, and in 1848. In any case, the popular appeal of chartism may not be reduced to episodic 'hunger politics'. As a campaigning movement for democratic rights and for an end to political exclusion, it maintained throughout a continuing presence and commitment which was independent of trade movements and of popular reactions to the state of the economy.

The verdict of historians of chartism in Scotland emphasises the mainly peaceful, rational and disciplined character of agitation and activism, and the relative absence of confrontation on both sides. In contrast, the agitation in England and Wales, and in Ireland, occasionally spilled over into violence and disorder, meeting with reprisals and arrests. However, if the course of chartism and of radical protest in Scotland during these years was relatively free from open violence, the inevitable question is posed as to why this was evidently the case north of the border. Clearly, this is a complex question which deserves greater investigation by historians, and one which is nowhere near resolution.

Considering the experience of chartism in Aberdeen, this historian is unable to offer the vicarious pleasure of sensational scenarios of open conflict and class warfare such as occurred in storm centres elsewhere. In Aberdeen, there was no insurrectionism; no arming; no confrontations between the military, police, and protesters; no rioting; no breaking up of meetings; and no arrests for sedition or for alleged use of inflammatory language. Instead, there was, on occasion, militant rhetoric from chartist spokesmen spouting the language of physical force often in inverse relation to the degree of political action and responsibility they were prepared to undertake—although this characteristic was not peculiar to Aberdeen! Only once, in the high tension summer of 1842, the sheriff had to place special constables on the alert, when it was expected that the unemployed, encouraged by some of the chartists, were about to roam through the streets in bands, intimidating people for food and money, or worse, resort to stealing and looting. This turned out to be a false alarm, as the clergy and the town council's relief committee took the matter in hand and proceeded to extend relief provision, thus defusing the situation. The military were called out for the only time, in 1848, to monitor the behaviour of the meal mobs during the grain shortages and inflated food prices of that year. Apparently, this did not have any bearing upon, or connection with the incidence of chartism, but belonged to an older tradition of protest, enforcing 'fair' prices and the 'moral economy' by means of popular riot against the grain merchants and their agents.

Unlike Glasgow, Aberdeen was not a centre of political and industrial unrest aroused by the trial and victimisation of the Glasgow cotton spinners and the protest campaign which followed on behalf of trade union rights and release of the accused men. It is impossible to gauge the extent of working-class indignation in Aberdeen on this issue. Locally, the cotton masters had for many years managed to prevent factory-based spinning from being a male preserve and thus, in contrast to Glasgow, their spinners were women and girls. The only surviving statement from working-class sources is contained in an interesting letter which appeared in the Edinburgh chartist newspaper, *True Scotsman*, in November 1838, where the Aberdeen branch of the union of operative masons defended the right of peaceful combination against the calumnies of a hostile press and establishment. Further, they stated their radical opposition to the existence of powerful self-interested combinations of ruling-class politicians, bankers, merchants, manufacturers, corn dealers, 'and last, though not least, the Established clergy' who all made life difficult for workers and trade unionists.

In further consideration of the peculiarities of the Aberdeen political scene, two important elements which contributed to extremism and the potential for disorder in other areas, were missing locally. Firstly, there was no militant Irish presence to swell the agitation for an end to atrocities in Ireland and/or for self-determination. The Irish dimension was important in the west of Scotland, not as a progressive force as yet, but as a focal point of sectarian division encouraged by Orange elements and employers who used the immigrant Irish as strike-breakers and blacklegs, particularly in mining communities. The issue did not arise in Aberdeen, where the Irish-born population, numbering just over 1,000, was evidently not conspicuous in active political life or in worker organisations. This did not mean that the Aberdeen chartists were apathetic on the question of Ireland. Indeed, they castigated the British government for policies of coercion, military repression and martial law in the tithe war of the 1830s, but did not allow stances on the Irish question to be confused with the principal thrust of chartist demands.

Secondly, in Aberdeen, there was no militant groundswell of opposition, as developed in the north of England, against the operation of the new poor law, the introduction of the workhouse system and the transfer of depressed people from the rural areas of the south to the industrial north, which was seen by so many workers there as a deliberate threat to their jobs and conditions. The system of poor relief in Scotland was different, and although it was by no means humane, it did not involve the imposition of a hated workhouse system. The Scottish poor law denied relief to the able bodied unemployed and proved to be an important grievance in Aberdeen, especially in 1842 and in 1848 when thousands of people were made redundant and impoverished. Local chartists, led by the young tailor James Shirron and the shoemaker David Wright, represented the unemployed in repeated appeals to the council and the clergy, claiming full maintenance and the right to work, in opposition to degrading, harsh discipline relief work schemes such as turf cutting on the links, stone breaking at Rubislaw quarry, and, in 1848, labour gangs on new drainage schemes. In that year, the chartists managed to organise successful resistance to the operation of such degrading relief schemes, but without forcing a fundamental change in the existing, mean, poor law system.

In Aberdeen, chartism was led by artisans—radical, craft-conscious journeymen—and, in the first phase, by a couple of small employers, namely Joseph Rowell and John McPherson who each owned a combworks. No factory workers can be identified among the local leadership or principal activists, although from 1839 onwards there existed a female chartist association which was composed mainly of textile workers who were active in a supporting rank and file capacity. Industrial capitalism in textiles had developed in and around the city from the end of the eighteenth century, and out of a population of 63,000 in 1841, rising to 72,000 by 1851, the woollen, linen and cotton industries employed up to 13,000 men, women and children. However, although dominated by textile manufacture, Aberdeen was far from being a single sector mill town. The city was a major commercial centre, involved in shipbuilding and in shipping. Six shipyards employed hundreds of wrights, carpenters and moulders; a growing machine engineering industry provided work for over 1,000 skilled and semi-skilled men in the busy mid 1840s; the two comb works employed 400 workers; and the various construction industries and trades were occupied with extensive building programmes throughout the city centre and the new west end.

However, the leading chartist spokesmen and activists did not come from better-paid occupations such as engineering, shipbuilding, or craft stoneworkers (John Legge, a journeyman mason, was an exception), but from occupations which were in decline and under severe pressure from capitalist re-organisation and competition. Traditional artisan occupations made up a large section of the labour force in the 1830s and 1840s, including a diminishing number of hand loom weavers, followed by around 800 boot and shoemakers and 500 tailors, all of which were struggling trades. Displaced artisans in the textile trades, such as flaxdresser Archibald Macdonald, were also among the leaders, although the hand loom weavers—desperate and depressed—do not appear to have produced known chartist activists. And although mill workers and artisans were conspicuous elements in the social structure of the city, there was also a large middle class in the mercantile, manufacturing, shopkeeping and professional sectors, indicating the variety of social development in this northern outpost of commercial and industrial capitalism.

In a brilliant polemical article, Stuart McCalman presented an uncompromising critique of the political mentality and disposition of the petit-bourgeois and plebeian radicals who were the leading lights of chartism in the city.[4] According to the classic Marxist formulation which is used, such was the objective class position of the independent, or once-independent, craftsman and small master under the pressure of encroaching industrial capitalism that he felt threatened by both the bourgeoisie on one hand and the new industrial proletariat on the other. Unable to fully identify with either of these class forces, when it came to the world of political decision-making the artisan was a typical vacillator, in the final resort being unable to break from the presence and ideological influence of the rising middle class. In times of political crisis, as in 1842 particularly, the weakness of the artisan was fully exposed, displaying a fear of the latent and real industrial and political strength of the industrial working class, and near paranoia about civil war or any disorderly disturbance or confrontation. Instead, this artisan leadership was doubly anxious to conduct an ag'tation which would impress and convince the middle class, and indeed the ruling class, who would see in the image of a law-abiding, respectable and disciplined radical agitation the worthiness of the case for conceding democratic political rights.

According to this argument, the consequence of this type of leadership was the turning of mass working-class support into a number of blind alleys, into accommodation or collaboration with the forces of the middle class as expressed in progressive liberalism; into the safety valve of hell-fire Christianity and religiosity through chartist church sermons; or into schemes of a social reformist or self-help nature which were a substitute for, and/or a diversion from, the primary task of mass political struggle and direct action. Moreover, this artisan radical mentality was backward looking, concerned to restore the fast-disappearing world of imagined stability and security enjoyed by the small master and independent craftsman of the era before industrial capitalism and the factory system, and before the objective growth of a large industrial proletariat with whom they had little in common as producers and in their expectations and life styles.

The typical artisan radical critique found the source of social evils and political inequality in the landed aristocracy and the ruling oligarchy which represented their narrow and nefarious interests. The aristocracy and their hangers-on—including many of the Church of Scotland clergy—were responsible for the perpetuation of reaction, waste and corruption, for the sinecures and pensions, the taxes on bread and on other necessities, and the tax on knowledge itself through the tax on newspapers. They were fomenters of wars, and the enemies of all honest, industrious people who produced the wealth of the country.

This was indeed the common currency and vocabulary of plebeian radicalism going back to the 1790s, and as far as may be determined from the available evidence, it was overwhelmingly typical of the radical outspokenness among the artisans and small masters of Aberdeen from 1815 right up to, and including, the period of chartism. This mentality was neither anti-capitalist nor republican, but contained levelling sentiments for the removal of the powers and privileges of the landed aristocracy, although views about the disposal of estate properties were unclear.

Written from a standpoint of revolutionary purism, McCalman's characterisation of the artisan leaders and of their ideology and political practice is convincing in an epigrammatic way, and the essence of his conclusions in this regard have already been endorsed and incorporated in my own writing. However, in his treatment of various features of the chartist experience, the approach is over-schematic, tending at times to be unduly dismissive in some of its assumptions. Some points of contention are worth raising here in the interests of clarification and further elaboration, especially with regard to the resourcefulness of the plebeian radical tradition which was carried into—and, arguably, bedevilled—chartist politics and perspectives; and to the strategic political options which were available—or closed—to chartist activists, as they perceived and grappled with them at different moments during the crucial decade.

For instance, in the years between 1832 and 1838, it is necessary to understand why the radical ideology of 'People versus Aristocracy and Establishment'—rather than notions of labour versus capital—was such a potent force, and not merely an ideological baggage inherited from the radical critique of 'Old Corruption', which ought somehow to have been thrown aside in favour of a modern, advanced class awareness and proto-socialist consciousness among chartist activists and their proletarian supporters. In other words, it seems to me, theories of 'false consciousness' are unhelpful to the historian.

Secondly, and not only in the Aberdeen context, it is important to explain and demonstrate the nature and appeal of the ideology and movements of the radical and reforming sections of the middle class, which actively competed with those of chartism and with any notions of independent working-class power or emancipation. Thirdly, it is important to appreciate fully the political difficulties which confronted and confounded the chartists after the adverse events of 1839, instead of using the advantage of hindsight to score easy points about the limitations of their conduct.

Fourthly, we cannot ignore certain features of chartist culture which tend to be treated as side-shows, particularly in those cases where new forms were tried out, and alternative values were sought, however imperfectly. Education for citizenship was an integral part of chartist aspirations and endeavours. It took several forms, including teetotalism, co-operative schemes, and the exercise of collective self-help; and such activities were not always hijacked by, or surrendered to, the control and provenance of middle-class reformers.

In this review, there is yet another problematic area which deserves close analysis, and that is the extent to which, in the crucial years 1839-42, popular and working-class energies and perceptions were absorbed by, or diverted into, the consuming controversy between Church and State in Scotland leading to the Disruption; and the identification of anti-Establishment feeling with anti-landlordism, anti-clericalism, popular evangelicalism, and the strident aspirations and efforts of the influential middle class to reform and control the Church and its educational and social welfare responsibilities in the crowded central areas of Aberdeen and other towns. Here, there is scope to use and build upon the approach and insights of Allan McLaren in his excellent book on the Disruption in Aberdeen.[5]

From the radical and chartist viewpoint in 1838, the landed aristocracy were still entrenched in power, and the Whig governments which were the beneficiaries of the 1832 reformed political system, had not only betrayed the reforming principles their spokesmen had once professed during the struggle for change in 1830-32, but since then they had ruled as an authoritarian, anti-working-class regime, responsible for a series of legislative and judicial attacks on civil liberties and rights, as well as on living conditions. They had also declared arrogantly against further political reform, thereby excluding the great majority of the people from direct participation and representation in political decision-making. However, burning resentment at the outrage of political exclusion, and the holding of radical convictions were not sufficient, on their own, to generate a large and sustained popular movement. By 1838, working-class grievances, and their politicisation into a co-ordinated movement provided the vital dimension for a mass campaign for basic rights, the political demands and lessons having been forged out of recent experiences of struggle for improved working and living conditions.

In 1834, the Aberdeen tailors and shoemakers had taken strike action on wages and conditions. At the same time they provided solidarity with female textile factory workers who rebelled against harsh work discipline, abuse, and wage cuts. This industrial action by over 1,000 women in the linen and thread mills lasted for five weeks. A Female Operative Union was formed and combined meetings with other sets of workers led to plans for forming general unions, in the spirit of the movement elsewhere in Britain to promote the Grand National Consolidated Trades Union. In Aberdeen, blackleg labour, and the Master and Servant Law were used against the workers who had broken their contracts of employment. Victimised workers were issued with discharge notes which ensured they would be blacklisted by other employers in the city and far beyond.

The beleaguered hand loom weavers, unable to compete against the power loom, and confronted by a 'combination of the masters' to keep down piece-work rates of wages, had petitioned their MP Alexander Bannerman, and had given evidence before two parliamentary commissions of enquiry. Their protests and representations were to no avail, and instead of achieving their objectives for restoration of paternalist legislation to protect a minimum wage, and imposition of a tax on power looms, Parliament and the textile employers abandoned them to their fate.

Thus, between 1834 and 1838, weavers, tailors, shoemakers, and female factory workers, among others, were coming to realise that their grievances would not be resolved by trade union action or by sectional means, which had resulted in defeats at the hands of the employers and class law. There is no doubt that this undercurrent of unrest and pent-up grievance fed into early support for the People's Charter. The demand for the Charter embodied the demand for a democratic regime which would sweep away oppressive class legislation and usher in new laws which would guarantee and protect working-class rights and decent conditions of life. The objectives and aspirations behind the Charter were revolutionary, and not only transcended the familiar critique of 'Old Corruption', but included class demands for the likes of press freedom, trade union rights, and political democracy.

There was every expectation that a concerted campaign of working class and popular mobilisation to exert pressure on Parliament would be a successful strategy. The expression of the general will of the people in a universally organised public opinion would be irresistible. It was widely believed that political demonstrations and mass pressure had been effective in wresting the 1832 reform settlement from a reluctant aristocracy. However, this time round, the chartists were determined to apply the lesson whereby a mass working-class agitation would not allow democratic demands to be compromised and liquidated as they had been in the agitations of 1830-32.

From June 1838, chartist efforts, through the Aberdeen Working Men's Association, were devoted to gaining mass support for the National Petition which was due for presentation before Parliament. The Association started an unstamped paper *Aberdeen Patriot* in November 1838, and organised a series of outdoor meetings. At one rally held in August on the Broadhill, at the links, an estimated crowd of 10,000 people demonstrated with bands and banners in a carnival atmosphere. By January 1838, 7,000 signatures had been collected from Aberdeen in support of the People's Charter, and, shortly afterwards, a further 1,600 were gathered to boost the national target figure of 2 million names.

Parliament rejected the National Petition in July 1839, and plunged the chartist movement into crisis. The Chartist Convention of delegates meeting in London, then in Birmingham, debated the next moves and recommended a month-long general strike, combined with abstention from alcohol and exclusive dealing, with the aim of putting pressure on government revenues. From reports, it would appear that neither Scotland generally, nor Aberdeen in particular was in favour of this drastic course of action. It was deemed unrealistic as well as dangerous. Already, a split had emerged over strategy and styles of agitation. In July, the Aberdeen chartist body debated the Convention's recommendations, including a resolution on the principle of arming for the purposes of self-defence. A majority declared in favour of this principle—the right of armed resistance to the forces of a tyrannical government—but a splinter group around the ex-shoemaker John Mitchell seceded from the Association. Mitchell and his followers in the new Artisans Association were adamant that rash talk of physical violence and ulterior measures like armed defence would play into the hands of reaction, and kill off any support that was likely to come from the progressive middle class. In his poem 'The Vision of Famine', Mitchell warned,

> Stand not the people on the horrid brink
> Of Insurrection?—war's dread archangel,
> With his blood red flag of conflagration.
> Have not your cities been in flames, lit by
> The rebel and the spy.

According to this opinion, discipline and reason was required to defeat the agent provocateur, and disown the advocates of violence and threats of violence.

From July 1839, the abortive Newport uprising and outbreaks of frustrated violence in several industrial areas alarmed the government into swift reprisals. Over 400 chartists, including the entire English leadership, were imprisoned on charges of sedition, incitement and illegal assembly. The movement was effectively decapitated for the time being, except in Scotland, where there were no arrests and no outbreaks of political violence. In Aberdeen, despite the wrangle over strategy, tactics, and future direction of the democratic movement, a remarkable united campaign was mounted in defence of the jailed chartists. Civil liberties protests involved fund raising, petitions, and public meetings.

However, from 1839, chartism was susceptible to middle-class pressure, especially in Aberdeen where there was a strong, vocal agitation for repeal of the Corn Laws and in favour of free trade legislation and further political reform. The Aberdeen Anti-Corn Law League was headed by James Adam, editor of the liberal-radical weekly paper *Aberdeen Herald*, which since 1832 had articulated these demands and had built up an influential body of public support behind them. The shipping magnate, George Thomson, Alexander and Thomas Bannerman and other prominent businessmen, non-conformist clergy and middle-class evangelicals were all active in this reforming movement. After successive defeats in Parliament over corn law and free trade issues, this middle-class lobby, by 1841, had turned to political agitation to mobilise popular support for a new movement to defeat the entrenched power of aristocracy and monopoly. This radical lobby took shape in the formation of the complete suffrage movement, which had branches in towns up and down the country.

In Aberdeen, the complete suffrage agitation was a serious rival to the chartists. Men such as John Mitchell and the pacifist wing of the chartist moderates had no trouble in identifying with it, as they had reconciled themselves to a long haul strategy of winning political change by contesting elections and merging with the radical middle class for this purpose. Nevertheless, the mainstream chartist body—re-organising under the leadership of Feargus O'Connor, released from prison at the end of 1841—maintained an independent line *vis-à-vis* the middle-class radicals and free traders, and was intransigent in its opposition to their attempts to head off and capture the reviving chartist agitation. The Aberdeen Charter Union, effectively the local branch of the National Charter Association (which may be regarded as the first nationally organised working-class political party in Britain) kept its agitational and organisational independence through late 1841 and into the middle of 1842, by which time the economy had collapsed, and working-class allegiance to the chartist cause had grown visibly. In contrast, the complete suffragists made good headway among the electors, but during late 1841 and in 1842, failed to forge a popular radical alliance with working-class support. Chartist opposition began, at this juncture, to develop a more marked class-conscious viewpoint, as the middle-class movement was seen to represent the interests of the employers, particularly the manufacturers, who were out for their own ends, including that of free trade which suited their economic interests, but conspicuously failed to convince industrial workers of the advantages to them in terms of improved wages and conditions. Indeed, the experience of wage cuts and redundancies in the depression of 1842 had the effect of hardening working-class opinion against the employers who were carrying out this rationalisation of labour, and removed the basis for a class alliance.

In the early months of 1842, the Aberdeen Charter Union was busy in signing up subscribing members and collecting signatures for the second National Petition. It had a full-time paid secretary and possessed funds to pay for visiting lecturers who supplemented the political education of the mutual instruction classes which had been organised since January to inform members and new recruits in the principles of democracy and citizenship. Aberdeen's contribution to the great petition was 17,000 names; and even when Parliament again rejected the Charter in May, the appeal of chartism continued to grow, reaching its peak in the summer months. Shipyard workers, iron moulders, masons, weavers, combmakers, and a host of factory workers—mainly women—became subscribing members, and attended crowded, animated political meetings, lectures and classes in the chartist premises at Queen Street and at 38 George Street. Outdoor meetings had to be held on the links in the summer evenings, as the existing halls and rooms could not cope with the clamour for political clarification and action.

By August, the course of events was dictated by rolling strikes and disturbances in industrial areas, particularly Lancashire and the raw mining communities of Lanarkshire. The National Charter Association had initially supported a call from a trades conference in Manchester to escalate this action into a political general strike for the Charter. This call was debated extensively in mid August at three meetings of delegates from the various trades affiliated and associated with the Aberdeen Charter Union. Eventually, a majority of 20 to 12 decided not to oppose the call, but in the meantime to await further developments.

The issue was decided for the local chartists, as the national leaders called off the proposed action, having had second thoughts about the consequences of a confrontation with the forces of the armed state. Some, like O'Connor, were convinced that the sudden lock-outs in the textile districts of the north of England was a ploy of the industrialists to provoke worker violence and state repression, to enable them subsequently to inflict wage cuts and harsher discipline.

The local chartist leaders were horrified by the reports of mob violence and attacks upon property in the troubled English areas. They were political radicals—not revolutionaries—whose perceptions on strategy were based upon the mobilisation of mass pressure and informed public opinion. Defeat of radical aspirations was certain unless the government failed to withstand this pressure, lost nerve, and conceded fundamental reforms. It stood firm, and the same dilemma facing the radical position was repeated in the 1848 crisis, except that on this later occasion, tragedy turned to farce, as Aberdeen was one of the chartist localities where it was reported—in statements encouraged by national leaders such as Ernest Jones and by local chartist spokesmen—that an armed people's militia had been mobilised in anticipation of government repression. Thus, it was not only the well-known historic event of 12 April 1848, when the last great mass chartist demonstration in London presented the final National Petition before Parliament, which ended in failure: the reputation of chartism as a responsible and serious political movement in Aberdeen failed to overcome the ridicule incurred by its leading spokesmen with their irresponsible talk of armed mobilisation. Opportunistic, militant rhetoric had helped to sabotage the movement, at a time when an honest, courageous appraisal of political realities—including alternative strategies of mobilisation and preparation—was imperative.

It is nevertheless important to re-emphasise that there was more to chartism than petitioning, the politics of the platform and the mass meeting, and direct mobilisation in demonstrations, whether local or national. In the years between 1838 and 1842 especially, building the cultural dimension of the radical movement was a real commitment, and should not be regarded as a peripheral or diversionary concern. Such commitments were complementary, and not antithetical, to the primacy of political struggle. Chartist culture was about preparation for exercise of the rights of citizenship in the democracy which would be ushered in following the enactment of the six points. To that extent, political expectations were high, and aspirations were revolutionary. In other words, the countervailing radical culture was hegemonic in its aspirations, and bound up with notions of an impending transformation of political rights and popular power. As Aberdeen exemplifies, the various means of building up confidence and resources for the political struggle included lectures; political education meetings; the reading aloud, and fervent debating, of articles and reports in the chartist press, particularly from the *Northern Star*; abstention from liquor pledges; the people's own, democratically organised chartist church. And all these activities were accompanied by an urgent moral earnestness, which helped build up confidence for the political struggle.

In their manifesto address of 1838, the Aberdeen Working Men's Association castigated the ruling class and the clergy for deliberately keeping the people in ignorance of their rights, denying a national system of education, and curbing the press. They boycotted the Mechanics Institute, on the grounds that it banned discussion of politics and religion, and functioned under the tutelage of the employers as a technical college instead of being a forum for free working-class education and critical debate. The chartist body made their own provision. In 1838, the Association had a small premises in Correction Wynd, where John Mitchell ran a shop, and sold the chartist and radical press. In 1839, it rented a larger centre at 41 Queen Street. Here, a mutual instruction class met weekly, and the premises functioned as a reading room, coffee room and temperance hall. It was also a venue for soirées with concerts of recitations of radical verse and hymn singing, including new radical compositions. Nearby was the first chartist church. In 1841, the Charter Union acquired lease of a hall in George Street, and at nearby no.48, John Legge, the chartist mason, ran a radical bookshop and stationery. For a while, he edited a local chartist news-sheet *The Northern Vindicator* although it, like the *Aberdeen Patriot*, apparently survived for only a couple of issues. In July 1842, at the height of chartist membership and appeal, the Aberdeen Charter Union decided to buy—not lease—a much larger premises as a radical political and educational centre. For £180 (a large sum of money in 1842) they bought a former school building in Blackfriars Street, which they proceeded gradually to renovate and extend to hold up to 1,800 people. Membership subscriptions and shares secured the initial payment for the premises, and, between 1843 and 1847, with some help from middle-class sympathisers, the new building was completed, having been in constant use for radical meetings, educational classes, and social activities.

After 1842, non-chartist involvement in the Blackfriars Street centre was already an indication that chartist cultural efforts had lost their dynamic as an independent activity, fragmented, and become susceptible to middle-class interference and patronage. The political initiative for radical reform passed to the middle-class liberals in the Complete Suffrage Association, and although the chartist organisation remained separate in name, its profile in the community was subordinate to that of the rising influence of radical and social reforming liberalism. This new consensus in the years 1843-47 was typified by the support and encouragement given to the political-cultural activities of Robert Lowery, formerly a nationally prominent moral force chartist who, in 1843, settled in Aberdeen. He proclaimed the principles and practice of radical Christianity from the pulpit of the old Relief church in St Andrews Street, combining this message with militant teetotalism and moral and educational reform. In 1844, he bought coffee rooms in Broad Street. The premises served as a total abstinence institute, and as a meeting place for discussion of political and social questions, as well as participation in dancing and singing. The whole atmosphere and purpose was bound up with the promotion of working-class respectability and educational and political gradualism which, in time, was to become the currency of mid Victorian liberal values. In 1843, John Mitchell, whose political viewpoint and style coincided with that of Lowery, started and ran, again with middle-class financial support, a popular radical liberal weekly newspaper, *Aberdeen Review*, which lasted until the end of 1844.

However, despite this collapse of mainstream chartist politics into the expanding milieu of popular liberal causes and concerns, three separate initiatives which were chartist-inspired and sustained were evidence of continuing working-class resourcefulness. Firstly, several leading chartists were also keen co-operators, and were instrumental, during the mid 1840s, in helping to revive an earlier interest in principles and schemes which held out the vision of an alternative social order, based upon building the co-operative commonwealth. In 1830, during the first flush of enthusiasm for the co-operative movement, Aberdeen pioneered eight branches with 900 members, engaged not only in managing and patronising retail shops, but in savings banks and in house-building investment. These schemes had collapsed in the depression years, and in the more favourable mid 1840s were organised afresh. The Aberdeen Association of Producers was started by chartist working men in 1844. Its store in the Gallowgate sold clothes, unadulterated food, and banned the sale of liquor on principle. It flourished, and established a savings bank for members in 1845. Its objectives were more economic than political, although the venture was intended to grow into a scheme of co-operative production through the creation of self and mutual employment as an alternative to capitalist control of labour and production. This body may have been involved in the co-operative meal mill, started in Bucksburn in 1848, known locally as 'the Chartists' mill'. The fate of the Aberdeen Association of Producers is not known, but it is likely that many of its members and adherents had an overlapping interest in other, concurrent collectivist schemes such as the chartist Land Plan and the National Association of United Trades.

Co-operative schemes—in which chartists played a prominent part in the 1840s—were directed against the political economy of capitalism. The National Association of United Trades—formed in 1845, and another chartist initiative—was also directed at countering the 'power of capital'. By 1848, this defensive organisation of trade unions had over 400 members in Aberdeen, including journeymen tailors, shoemakers, bakers, iron moulders, causeway stone makers, tinsmiths, pipemakers, carpet weavers, tape weavers and combmakers. Its objectives were political and industrial, leading to the emancipation of labour. The immediate effort lay in united labour organisation to prevent and campaign against sweated labour, low wages, subcontracting, and unemployment. They were also interested in promoting schemes of co-operative production, but none appear to have been started in Aberdeen, and the United Trades did not survive the economic and political storms of 1848. Neither did the Aberdeen Land Company, which had been founded in 1845 to promote the chartist Land Plan. This scheme attracted a lot of interest among workers in Aberdeen, although only a few bought up shares at £1. 6s. each, or paid instalments towards the scheme. Again, the vision was anti-capitalist—one of small holding colonies, agrarian self-sufficiency in healthy surroundings, free from the despotism of the factory, the sweat shop, and urban squalor and poverty. For those in Aberdeen who pinned their hopes on the abortive land scheme, the outcome was a cruel deception. The Chartist Land Company, mismanaged by Feargus O'Connor, collapsed in 1848, amid recriminations and a parliamentary enquiry, and although the social vision contained in land plan objectives helped to sustain political interest during the 'lean years' of chartist activity, it was a chimera and a political blind alley which damaged an otherwise highly resourceful working-class movement for democratic rights.

NOTES

1. This article is based on Robert E. Duncan, 'Popular Radicalism and Working Class Movements in Aberdeen 1790-1850' (unpublished M.Litt. thesis, Aberdeen University, 1976); and his 'Artisans and Proletarians: Chartism and working class allegiance in Aberdeen 1838-1842', *Northern Scotland*, IV (1981), 51-67. See also his *Textiles and Toil: The Factory System and the Industrial Working Class in Early 19th Century Aberdeen* (Aberdeen, 1984).
2. Leslie C. Wright, *Scottish Chartism* (Edinburgh, 1953); Alexander Wilson, *The Chartist Movement in Scotland* (Manchester, 1970).
3. See the 'note on further reading' which follows.
4. Stuart McCalman, 'Chartism in Aberdeen', *Journal of the Scottish Labour History Society*, 2 (April, 1970), 5-24.
5. A. Allan MacLaren, *Religion and Social Class: the Disruption Years in Aberdeen* (London, 1974).

Note on Further Reading

The standard work on chartism as a whole is now Dorothy Thompson, *The Chartists: Popular Politics in the Industrial Revolution* (pbk edn., Aldershot, 1986). On Scotland Alexander Wilson, *The Chartist Movement in Scotland* (Manchester, 1970) has not yet been replaced. For a comprehensive bibliography up to the date of publication, see *Bibliography of The Chartist Movement, 1837-1976* ed. J.F.C. Harrison and D. Thompson (Hassocks, 1978).

Recent stimulating historical studies which deal with the contest for control over working class leisure time and cultural provision, and demonstrate that this was an ideological (and sometimes physical) battleground include the following: *Working Class Culture: Studies in History and Theory* ed. John Clarke, Chas Critcher and Richard Johnson (London, 1979), especially chapter 3 by Johnson, 'Really Useful Knowledge: radical education and working class culture 1790-1848'; a pioneering article by Elspeth King, 'Popular Culture in Glasgow' in *The Working Class in Glasgow 1750-1914* ed. R.A. Cage (London, 1987); and *The Chartist Experience: Studies in Working Class Radicalism and Culture 1830-1860* ed. J. Epstein and D. Thompson (London, 1982), especially Epstein's case study of Nottingham, showing the centrality of the chartist struggle for cultural hegemony.

On the debate concerning popular radical and chartist articulation of class and perceptions of political strategy, a seminal article is 'Re-thinking Chartism', by Gareth Stedman Jones, chapter 3 of his *Languages of Class: Studies in English Working Class History 1832-1982* (Cambridge, 1983). An abridged version of this essay appears in *The Chartist Experience*. For a thorough, penetrating critique of Jones' conclusions on chartist articulation of class, it is worth consulting the review essay by Dorothy Thompson, 'The Languages of Class', in *Bulletin of the Society for the Study of Labour History*, 52 (1) (1987), 54-7.

In the context of defining the nature of radicalism and class politics and formation in early nineteenth-century Scotland, Tony Clarke and Tony Dickson review the state of the debate in a useful article 'The Birth of Class?', in *People and Society in Scotland 1760-1830*, I (Edinburgh, 1988) ed. Tom Devine and Rosalind Michison (Edinburgh, 1988), 292-309.

6 THE RED CLYDESIDERS AND THE SCOTTISH POLITICAL TRADITION

William Knox

The sweeping victory of November 1922, which saw Labour win ten of Glasgow's fifteen parliamentary divisions, generated an enthusiasm in the city that bordered on the millennial. Mass meetings to celebrate the electoral triumph were held all over Glasgow. On Sunday 20 November at St Andrews Hall a service of dedication was held at which the audience sang the covenanting 23rd and 124th psalms—'Had not the Lord been on our side'—and Rosslyn Mitchell, a convert from the Liberal Party, drafted a declaration to which the newly elected MPs publicly pledged themselves to 'abjure vanity and self-aggrandizement' and to recognise 'that their only righteous purpose is to promote the welfare of their fellow citizens and the well-being of mankind'. The climax to the celebrations was the rousing send off the victorious Clydeside MPs received at St Enoch's Station. Around 250,000 people packed the surrounding streets to see them off to London. The scene was almost biblical. The crowd sang some old Scots songs, 'Jerusalem', and finished with 'The Red Flag' and the 'Internationale'. As Emanuel Shinwell recalled in his autobiography, the Glasgow workers had 'a frightening faith in us. We had been elected because it was believed we could perform miracles'.[1]

The events and the language surrounding the celebrations throw up a series of interesting questions about the nature of Labour politics in Scotland at this time. Who were the Red Clydesiders? Who did they represent politically? What was the nature of their political philosophy and what was the value system they operated within? Finally, what caused the messianic zeal, so vividly captured in the events of November 1922, to dissipate itself and lead to the disaffiliation of the Independent Labour Party (ILP) in 1932, and what impact did this event have on the future ethos and political philosophy of the Labour Party in Scotland?

One of the most enduring political myths is that the Labour Party is the party of the working class. While it is undoubtedly true that the party has historically gained most of its electoral support from the working class, the leadership of the organisation has been more socially heterogeneous. Indeed, the Scottish ILP was a product of a social alliance between the petit- bourgeoisie and skilled workers and this reflected in the occupational backgrounds of those Labour MPs elected in 1922. Some like James Maxton were school teachers, others like John Wheatley were businessmen, and a few were skilled workers like David Kirkwood and John Muir who had come to prominence during the wartime struggles on Clydeside. This maintained a social pattern that had been established as far back as the socialist revival of the 1880s. The founding members of the Scottish Labour Party and the more Marxist socialist organisations such as the Social Democratic Party and the Socialist League all displayed similar class profiles regarding their leadership.[2]

What made this social alliance possible was the operation of a shared value system derived from the ethos of popular liberalism and subscription to the culture of respectability. Socially, labour leaders like Keir Hardie were teetotal, rational, untheoretical and evangelical in religion; politically, they were radical, republican, anti-landlord and nationalist. Their heroes were Jesus, Shelley, Mazzini, Whitman, Carlyle and Burns.[3] Of the Clydesiders, John Paton, ILP national organiser, claimed that the most formative political/literary influences were the works of Burns and the inspiration of the Bible.[4] More recent research would also add the names of Marx, Hardie and William Morris to Paton's list.[5] What connected the conservative thinker, Carlyle, and the social revolutionary, Marx, was that both had written savage critiques of the social consequences of the industrial revolution. Marx's *Capital*, Carlyle's *Past and Present*, and Morris' *Art and Labour* all condemned the soulless monotony of factory life; the ugliness and brutality of urban life; the exploitation of people and the environment for personal gain; and each in its own way offered a vision of a more humane and beautiful society. The Bible and the poetry of Burns complemented the vision of the social theorists by emphasising the equality and brotherhood of man; the former before God, and the latter in nature.

The possibility of raising society to a new plane on which ugliness would be replaced by beauty, competition by co-operation, was of crucial importance to human beings forced to endure or, in the case of the better off, to witness, the misery and squalor of much of working-class life in Scotland. And nowhere were these social problems better exemplified than in the area of housing. The Census of 1911 showed that 'over 62 per cent of Glasgow's population lived in one or two roomed dwellings', and the Sankey Commission of 1919 highlighted the wretched housing conditions in the mining villages of central Scotland.[6] In spite of the petit-bourgeois and skilled background of the Clydeside MPs all had first hand experience of the squalor and poverty of Scottish workers. The export orientation of the heavy industries of the west of Scotland made the economy vulnerable to shifts in world demand and led to short term unemployment among skilled tradesmen. Those MPs who were school teachers witnessed the poverty of Glasgow children on a daily basis and were appalled at the destitution. Maxton provides a graphic description of conditions at St James School, Bridgeton, when he claimed 'In the class I was teaching I had a class of sixty boys and girls of about eleven years of age ... thirty-six out of the sixty could not bring both heels and knees together because of rickety malformations'.[7] Those fortunate not to have personal experience of poverty came into contact with it as members of Glasgow Town Council, the parish councils and the education authorities. Thus it was desire to alleviate or abolish poverty which was the central political goal of the

Clydesiders rather than the restructuring of social relationships as Marxists would have desired.

Poverty was dependent on a political solution but the poor had to be raised morally as well as physically if they were to be fit and proper persons for the socialist commonwealth. The leadership of the Scottish labour movement was steeped in the culture of respectability which was intertwined with temperance, religion and education and manifested itself in attitudes towards popular culture and the socially unacceptable behaviour which underpinned it. Almost all of the Clydeside MPs were teetotal and some had organisational links with temperance organisations. In fact, the first piece of legislation the Clydeside MPs voted for in the Commons was the Liquor Traffic Control Bill, introduced by the temperance MP for Dundee, Edwin Scrymgeour. It included such draconian measures as the immediate closure of all public houses and five years' imprisonment for trafficking in liquor.[8] *Forward*—the mouthpiece of the Glasgow ILP—refused to accept adverts from the drinks trade and constantly preached prohibition even when the rest of the labour movement had seen it as unrealistic. Its enduring influence in the ILP was because it was an elemental part of the process of self-definition among the leadership and an essential instrument for creating a working class in the former's image. Politically, it meant that analysis of the social and economic condition of the Scottish working class was tinged with moralism. Labour leaders like Patrick Dollan in 1923 saw alcohol as 'one of the greatest obstacles to mass intelligence'; and six years later Rosslyn Mitchell could argue with solid conviction that alcohol was 'the greatest obstacle to reform that exists' and was responsible for 'everything; slums, crime, poverty, ill-health, public corruption, and sorrow to women and children'.[9]

Booze was not part of acceptable social behaviour for Clydesiders and this was extended to other forms of popular culture. Jazz, dance halls and cinemas were compared in the columns of *Forward* to 'opium dens' of yesterday.[10] Workers were encouraged to participate in wholesome entertainments and healthy pursuits. To this end socialist art circles and choirs were set up alongside the rambling clubs, the cycle scouts and football leagues and the various vocational classes and study groups. The hoped for outcome of these social initiatives was the creation of a sober, respectable and civilised working class refined in art and literature; clean in body and mind through temperance and outdoor pursuits—the social ideal of Gladstonian Liberalism.

Religion also had a part to play in defining the leadership and influencing the style and content of Scottish labour politics. The non-established churches claimed a substantial number of adherents among Scottish labour leaders mainly because, unlike the Church of Scotland, their ministry and laity were drawn from the small business and artisanal sections of society.[11] Locked out of the corridors of power, if not wealth, members of the non-established churches took a more socially critical view of the institutions of capitalist society. However, as religion emphasises the social message of the rich helping the poor; the strong the weak, its influence tended to obscure the class message of the labour movement. Few, if any, of the Clydesiders accepted Marx's materialist concept of history, even those like Neil Maclean, William

Leonard and James Maxton, who had acted as tutors in John Maclean's Marxist economics classes. Man was more spirit to them than the product of changing material circumstances. Clinging to religious or quasi-religious views, it was difficult for a class analysis of Scottish society to emerge among sections of the west of Scotland labour movement. The struggle was depicted as being between good and evil; of fairness and decency against rapaciousness and exploitation.

In spite of the weakness of the analysis, religion infused Labour with a moral zeal which was important in maintaining a level of political commitment. However the influence was not always positive. Progressive social reform was obstructed through the influence of religion on the Clydesiders. The winning of the Catholic vote in Glasgow was conditional on maintaining an opposition or silence on issues connected with birth control, abortion and segregated schooling, indeed anything calculated to harm the interests of the church. *Forward* refused to take adverts from advocates of birth control. Maxton, rather than recognise the liberating potential birth control held for women, allowing them to play an active part in society and the labour movement, advocated the 'intelligent control of the appetites and desires'.[12] All the Clydesiders operated around the notion of the male as breadwinner and the female as housekeeper and mother. Capitalism was attacked by the Clydesiders because it 'played havoc with the rich blessings of family life'.[13]

Therefore, although the Clydesiders were thought of as wild men, the evidence would point to another interpretation, one which would place stress on the conventionality and social conservatism of their world view. It would also emphasise their remoteness from the working class. Indeed, the class alliance that made up the Scottish ILP operated around the traditional values of the Scottish radical political tradition: teetotalism, pacifism, republicanism and morality. They were the twentieth century's embodiment of the spirit of the covenanters, and often referred to themselves as such. As John Paton put it, 'All of them could and did claim to be "rebels" against evil social conditions and the inequalities and injustices of Capitalism, but not one of them could it be said in any literal sense that he was a "revolutionary"'.[14] As the twentieth century wore on this was more than borne out. David Kirkwood, the revolutionary shop steward of the Clyde, became the first baron of Bearsden, Patrick Dollan accepted a knighthood in 1941, honorary doctrates and other awards were showered on Tom Johnston, George Buchanan was Minister of Pensions in the Attlee government, others like Agnes Dollan found their way into the Moral Re-armament Movement of the 1950s and 1960s. Only Maxton and Wheatley held aloof from the embrace of liberal capitalism. The majority of them who had set out to change society in 1922 had become incorporated into the capitalist system. The social profile and the value system provide the preconditions for incorporation but ultimately this phenomenon has to be explained at the level of politics.

What provided the Clydesiders with their wild image was their impatience with the parliamentary system and the slow pace of social reform. They were in a hurry; the poverty of their constituents meant that they could not be anything else. But what to do about it? In spite of victory in 1922 Labour was still a minority party in Westminster and was to remain so until 1945. What was the correct political tactic to pursue in this situation, where in spite of being able to form a government in 1924 and again in 1929 Labour was still dependent on the support of the other political parties to get legislation through the Commons? This issue was to provoke different responses from the various wings of the labour movement and was eventually to split the Labour Party leading to the disaffiliation of the ILP in 1932.

The MacDonald leadership wished to make Labour a respectable part of the mainstream of the British political system. This meant conciliating the middle classes and pursuing a moderate programme of social reform. The problem was that MacDonald's strategy and his emotional attachment to parliament was incomprehensible to the likes of Kirkwood, Maxton and Wheatley, who tended to view parliament as 'territory occupied by the class enemy'.[15] MacDonald's stress on the primacy of parliamentary politics over other forms of political or industrial protest also alienated the Clydesiders. Coming from Glasgow, and having taken part in the industrial and political struggles of the war years, men like Maxton and Wheatley stood out against the traditional separate spheres policy of the ILP. They spoke often on the need to supplement parliamentary activity with extra-parliamentary forms of protest. Maxton himself was convinced that 'capitalism [could be brought] to its knees by a well organised standstill ... in a few weeks'.[16] Thus the war on behalf of the poor was to be fought on a number of fronts. It was also to include all sections of the labour movement including Communists. The left continually campaigned for Communist affiliation to the Labour Party and, when the latter rebuffed the Communist embrace, worked with them in a series of joint campaigns, such as the National Left Wing Movement, designed to change the political direction of Labour.

The problem for the left was that there was a lack of unity among the Clydeside ILP over political strategy. An important part of the leadership grouped around people like Shinwell, Johnston and Dollan were emotionally and politically attached to MacDonald and his political practice. MacDonald had endeared himself to the Clydeside ILP by his opposition to the war and by his frequent visits to Glasgow, and through his weekly column in *Forward*. This axis also shared MacDonald's stress on the primacy of politics. During the short-lived Labour government of 1923-24, which increasingly drew criticism from even warm supporters, Dollan defended MacDonald in the pages of *Forward*, claiming that 'No man has worked harder for any cause than MacDonald has worked for the Socialism of the ILP'.[17] Dollan also criticised the idea of extra-parliamentary protest and argued that the 'walls of Capitalism are more likely to collapse as a result of the patient sapping and organised efforts of the ILP'.[18] As Communists were the foremost proponents of extra-parliamentary struggles Dollan opposed their affiliation to the Labour Party and was instrumental in pulling the Scottish ILP and the Glasgow Trades Council round to this view.

However, in the period prior to the General Strike the Clydeside left's views seemed more in step with the rank-and-file than those grouped around MacDonald. The ILP left successfully removed Clifford Allan, a close associate of MacDonald, as chairperson of the party, and then had the latter removed from the editorship of the ILP's theoretical journal, *Socialist Review*. Maxton was elected with an overwhelming number of votes as the new chairman of the ILP at its 1926 Easter conference. As a consequence of this there was imposition of greater discipline on the ILP parliamentary group, new guidelines for the selection of parliamentary candidates, and the adoption of a radical new economic strategy—'Socialism in our Time' (SIOT)—based on the underconsumptionist theories of J.A. Hobson, the liberal economist. On the industrial front, the success of 'Red Friday' in 1925, and the leftward move of the trade unions, seemed to herald a new mood of optimism and a rejection of the moderate policies of MacDonald. The General Strike changed all that, but the writing was on the wall prior to May 1926. The problem for the Clydeside left was that they could not read the writing.

Until Maxton's election as chairman, the ILP had pursued a 'separate spheres' policy, and this had denied it a base within the trade union movement. This meant the ILP was incapable of drawing support from this crucial part of the labour movement—something which was clearly demonstrated in its failure to win the support of the unions for the SIOT programme. Within the ILP there was a fundamental weakness undermining the left's political strategy. As the Labour Party was seen as a party of government it was natural that the politically aspiring should gravitate towards the locus of power and patronage and with Maxton as chairman of the ILP it ceased to be found there. At the time of Maxton's election the number of branches stood at 1,075 just three years later it had fallen to 746 and decline was occurring in every Divisional Council of the ILP. What increased the squeeze on the ILP was the fact that the Communists were a serious rival for the dissident left wing elements in the labour movement. The ILP could no longer claim to be the natural home of the left. But in the excitement generated by the General Strike this went unacknowledged as the labour movement pulled briefly together to defend the miners.

The failure of the General Strike witnessed the triumph of parliamentarianism over direct action. Syndicalist ideas which had considerable influence in the labour movement from before the First World War were effectively expunged from the vocabulary of the labour movement. It was to be parliament and not the industrial struggle which was to be the future motive force in bringing about economic and social justice. Ramsay MacDonald summed up the new political direction of the labour movement when he declared that 'the weapon of the General Strike is no good—even less now than ever'.[19] This conflicted with the interpretation of the left, who saw defeat as marking not the end of mass working-class action, but its beginning. Maxton, for example, saw defeat and the government repression which followed it, including the Trades Disputes Act of 1927, which outlawed the 'general' or 'sympathetic' strike, the Unemployed Insurance Act, which threatened to cut benefit to those claimants 'not genuinely seeking work', and the continued harassment of Communists, as creating conditions which 'made revolution inevitable'.[20] Therefore, the more repressive the government's actions, the more it would become apparent to the working class that capitalism was not in its interest. However, while the Clydeside left was determined to maintain the same mood of militancy which led to the General Strike, the trade union leaders had other ideas.

Faced with falling income and membership, the trade unions adopted a more collaborationist policy towards capital. The new approach was symbolised in the Mond/Turner talks of 1927-28 in which unions and management agreed to co-operate on a range of issues such as rationalisation, conciliation in industrial disputes and so on. The response to collaboration was the publication by the left of the Cook/Maxton manifesto of 1928, which called for the working class to engage in an unceasing war against capitalism and the Mond/Turner talks. It was an action which represented a decisive break in the increasingly fragile unity of the Clydeside ILP. The manifesto was published without consultation with the party or its National Administrative Council (NAC) and as such it came in for stinging rebukes from leaders such as Shinwell and Dollan. What concerned them most was the decision to act outside the party and to call 'unofficial conferences' with non-party members, most notably Communists,[21] to publicise the manifesto. The fact that at these meetings pledge cards were issued to those in attendance seems to suggest that a register of people who believed in the project was being compiled with the idea of moving towards an alternative leadership to that of MacDonald, or the creation of a new party. What is certain is that to many observers, partial or objective, the ILP was becoming a party within a party. As it was the ILP was a party split between those loyal to MacDonald and those who supported SIOT and were either critical or in outright opposition to the Labour leadership. And as the ILP tightened its grip on its parliamentary group to ensure it spoke with coherence on agreed conference decisions even if it meant going against Labour Party policy then speculation gave way to certainty. The ILP *was* a party within a party.

The experience of the 1929 Labour government finally convinced the left in the ILP that Labour was simply another party of social reform. It showed itself incapable of dealing with the problems of economic depression and mass unemployment. The Labour chancellor, Philip Snowden, pursued an economic strategy based on treasury orthodoxy and responded to the depression by cutting public expenditure. The actions of Labour were opposed all down the line by Maxton and other Clydeside MPs and they were able to force all night sittings on socially more objectionable legislation, such as the Anomalies Bill of 1931, which, under the name of economies, was to disqualify casual workers and married women from receiving unemployment benefit. Acting with MacDonald's blessing, Shinwell in parliament tried to silence Maxton, as Dollan did within the ILP. ILP parliamentary group meetings were packed with supporters of the government in spite of the fact that most, although nominally members, had not attended meetings for years. When that failed, the PLP passed a resolution forbidding MPs to vote against government legislation. Dollan effectively convinced the Scottish ILP Conferences to condemn the actions of the Maxton group in opposing government legislation, but failed to convince the NAC or the majority of Divisional Councils. The manoeuvring was ended when in 1930 annual conference supported a resolution supporting the restructuring of the ILP parliamentary group which would end all attempts to emasculate Maxton in the Commons. The resolution made the ILP group an autonomous body similar to the PLP which was unacceptable to the latter as it would have effectively undermined its authority within the Commons and the party.

Although negotiations carried on for some time with little movement from either side, the fall of the Labour government and the electoral debacle which followed saw the majority of the ILP vote to disaffiliate from the Labour Party in 1932. As far as Maxton was concerned, staying in the latter meant 'creating in the public mind the idea that the capitalist system in all its essentials must be preserved at all costs'.[22] The party, founded by Keir Hardie thirty-nine years before to unite the labour movement around the idea of independent labour representation, was now irredeemably split. Those still sympathetic to the Labour Party, such as Johnston and Dollan, founded the Scottish Socialist Party (SSP) affiliated to the Labour Party but devoted to the idea of continuing the work of the old ILP. Speaking on behalf of the new ILP, Maxton believed that he, given the existence of mass unemployment, would be able to achieve a parliamentary majority for socialism within five years.[23] However, in spite of the optimism, all that lay in store was political oblivion. Why had the messianic zeal of 1922 dissipated itself within ten years? What were the consequences of this for labour politics in Scotland?

Until 1922 the ILP had been united on the universal desire to make inroads into the hegemony of the Liberal Party in Glasgow and to solve the problem of poverty. The first wish was achieved in 1922 in Labour's historic victory; the second was more problematic. Electoral success held out the possibility that something concrete might be done towards solving the problem of poverty. Optimism had been based on past experience in municipal politics. Glasgow had been the centre of what *The Times* had deemed *the* experiment in municipal socialism. Municipal control had been established in wide areas of social and economic life, including telephones, tramways, wash houses, and much more besides. There were also a number of social initiatives to alleviate poverty such as free clothing and meals for needy children and feeding centres for the unemployed. It was reasonable to expect that Parliament would be no less responsive to the needs of the poor. However, that was not to be the case. Labour was always dependent on the support of some other party to get its legislative programme through Parliament, and while this had also been the case on the Glasgow Town Council, the Liberals were not as radical in the Commons as they were in Scotland. Frustration was increased by the lack of radicalism shown by successive Labour governments. Increasingly it seemed to the more radical members of the Clydeside ILP that the only way of dealing with poverty and unemployment was the removal of the MacDonald leadership and the replacement of gradualism with the more dynamic SIOT strategy. While the more moderate members of the Clydesiders might go some way with a more radical economic programme, if the price to be paid was the splitting of the Labour Party, then it was party first. Thus, for the moderates, it was party before class, while the left took the opposite view. These tensions finally came to a head during the lifetime of the second

Labour government when it was realised that cohabitation was no longer possible as the gap between the political wings of the party widened enormously. As so often in politics success brought its problems. When the emotion and rhetoric had to give way to the realities of parliamentary politics, the political language of compromise was anathema to the more radical. Whether the disaffiliationists' actions were mistaken is not our concern, but what is of concern is the impact disaffiliation had on the ethos and political philosophy of Labour in Scotland.

The disaffiliation of the ILP in 1932 marked a turning point in the political development of Labour and the political tradition of which it was a part. The growth of the Labour Party in Scotland took place within an ethos dominated by the precepts of popular liberalism. Socially, this was expressed through the influence of temperance and ethical religion; politically, its expression was found in a faith in ordinary people to control and shape their destiny. After 1932 this ethos collapsed as the labour movement became incorporated into the state. In the process the labour movement became more prone to middle-class ideologies and to rely on the bureaucrat and the planner rather than the people. The career of Tom Johnston illustrates the process. Johnston had been the founder and editor of *Forward* and part of the anti-war movement on Clydeside. He was deeply committed to the idea of home rule for Scotland and had supported George Buchanan's Government of Scotland Bill in 1924, and James Barr's Bill of 1927 which demanded dominion status for Scotland and the removal of Scottish MPs from Westminster. During the 1930s his position on home rule underwent a radical revision. His experiences in the Labour government of 1929-31 convinced him that important political issues had to be tackled in an atmosphere free from partisan political strife. Unemployed relief schemes was one of these issues and Johnston tried to get unemployment treated as an all-party question. Later in the decade Scottish affairs became another. Following a visit to the Soviet Union in 1935, he also became optimistic to the possibilities of economic and social planning. Thus in the 1930s the new basis of a political philosophy was mapped out: the regeneration of Scotland's economy and social life, through the application of physical planning and economic growth, and the drawing together of all sections of the Scottish community to provide a consensus on which the country's problems could be confronted.

Johnston's new position on home rule manifested itself in membership of a number of organisations, including the pro-planning 'Next Five Years Group' and the London Scots Self-Government Committee. The Committee was a radical nationalist body with a strong emphasis on planning: Johnston accepted the planning but rejected the radicalism. His new allies were to be found among what Christopher Harvie has called 'inter-party middle opinion groups' who 'sought social reconstruction through bipartisan policies of physical planning and economic growth'.[24] Thus although a member of the Self-Government Committee Johnston remained aloof from its actual operations, and the extent of his enthusiasm can be measured from the fact that while serving on the 1936-37 Gilmour Committee on Scottish administration he only went as far as to support the idea of a rationalisation of Scottish departments. By the time Johnston took office as Secretary of State for Scotland in 1941 his home rule programme involved no more 'than increased administrative autonomy, the segregation of Scottish business in parliament and the development of *ad hoc* executive and consultative bodies'.[25] Accompanying Johnston's move towards a more conservative view of home rule was a change in emphasis on the way it was to be attained. Like all the Clydesiders, Johnston had canvassed popular support for home rule among the electorate and members of the labour movement; from the 1930s he supported a more authoritarian approach in which those in power would bring some form of devolution to the Scottish people in spite of themselves.

As Labour in Scotland became increasingly drawn into the state and in the process become more authoritarian and conservative, it also lost its commitment to the pacifism which had encouraged its association with the reputation of the 'Red Clydesiders'. Pacifism was one of the political principles the Scottish ILP was founded upon and was most closely identified with the stand of Keir Hardie against the Boer War and imperialism, something he shared with radical Liberals. Hardie's clarion call for 'no alliances, no increased armaments, no interventions in the Balkans ... fraternity with the workers of the world'[26] influenced the Glasgow ILP in its opposition to the First World War. The ILP and other socialist organisations carried out anti-war campaigns which landed a number of them, such as Dollan, Maxton, Muir, Maclean, and others, in gaol on charges of sedition. It was their stand against the war which brought them to national attention and their experience was reflected in repeated demands for disarmament and the nationalisation of the armaments industry. In spite of the splits in the Labour Party in the early 1930s, Labour in Scotland continued to claim itself as a party of peace. Dollan, in his capacity as the first chairperson of the SSP, re-affirmed that it was an 'anti-war party' and that 'It would use all its propaganda influence against war and preparations for war'. There would, he declared, 'be 1,000 conscientious objectors in Scotland for the next war for every score in 1914'.[27] By 1938 Dollan was responsible for converting the Glasgow labour movement to the acceptance of civil defence and Air Raid Precautions. He also supported Chamberlain's 1938 National Voluntary Service Scheme. By the time of the outbreak of war in September 1939 the Scottish labour movement was solidly behind the war effort and the pacifist tradition lay with a minority in the SSP, the ILP and those members of the Labour Party in the Hardie tradition.

The rejection of pacifism was accompanied by the integration of Labour and the unions into a wartime version of the corporate state. Many of the leading anti-war personalities of the First World War recanted and like Arthur Woodburn, secretary of the Labour Party in Scotland, admitted that their past pacifist activities had been 'mistaken'.[28] Because of their valuable contribution to the war effort a number of Labour leaders were showered with honours and awards. Moreover, wartime membership of government boards and committees and, for some, directorships of public and private companies led to extensive ties with industry and commerce. Sir Patrick Dollan's post-war career reflects this process of incorporation. He became chairperson of the Scottish Advisory Committee for Civil Aviation, a director of British

European Airways, chairperson of the Scottish Fuel Efficiency Committee and
a member of the National Industrial Fuel Efficiency Board, chairperson of the
East Kilbride New Town Development Corporation and an executive member
of the Town Planning Association, manager of the Trustees Savings Bank in
Scotland, as well as a member and chairperson of a host of other organisations.[29] This list is by no means exhaustive; and a similar one could be
drawn up for comparable figures. Although the decline of pacifist sentiment
was not the progenitor of this process of incorporation, it was symptomatic
of the decreasing influence of the idealism associated with Marx, Morris,
Hardie, Burns, and of the values of popular liberalism. The older tradition
had its weaknesses, perhaps crucial weaknesses. It was based on a hybrid
morality associated with elitism and social puritanism, yet it also possessed
an emotional zeal to confront the evils of industrial capitalism. This strength
has to be contrasted with the blander professionalism of the labour movement
which developed in the 1930s.

   Among those who remained in the ILP and retained their idealistic sense
of transformation, the old ethos and tradition fared no better. From disaffiliation to political extinction the ILP became more London based, in spite
of the fact that the party's four MPs—Maxton, Buchanan, Stephen and
McGovern—all represented Glasgow constituencies. It also became more
internationalist and committed to ideas of class struggle. Maxton, who had
once been a member of the Scottish Home Rule Association, and had declared
that 'He would ask for no greater task in life than to make the English-
ridden, capitalist-ridden, landlord-ridden Scotland into a free Scottish Socialist
Commonwealth',[30] became anti-home rule in the 1930s. By 1932 he had
become convinced that the 'time had gone past for purely Nationalist struggles. A struggle for National independence and against imperialism can only
be fully justified if it combines with it a struggle for the overthrow of capitalism
as well'.[31] Waging the class war led to a disenchantment with Parliament
and a greater emphasis on workers councils as the transforming agent of
society. Maxton saw one of the tasks of the ILP as that of disabusing the
working class of the idea that 'Parliament alone would bring about the
establishment of a Socialist state'.[32] Thus the experience of the 1930s convinced those grouped around Maxton that past political practice had to be
revised and this involved a reformulation of the traditional roles ascribed by
the Scottish labour movement to education and parliamentary politics in
bringing about change in society. The whole edifice on which the ILP in
Scotland had been built upon from the time of Keir Hardie was swept away
and a political practice rooted in the Marxist concept of class struggle took
its place. Labour was divided fundamentally between two models of change;
revolution or Keynesian-style social reform. The victory of either meant a
wholesale transformation in the political tradition from which Labour had
emerged.

   The expectations of the Glasgow working class following the 1922 general
election were never realised. Parliament proved unresponsive to convictions
that at heart were emotional rather than intellectual. The wild men who set
off in haste to bring about change in the way the social and economic affairs

of the country were run were themselves changed. Only a few such as Maxton, Wheatley, and, for a time, Stephen, Buchanan and Kirkwood, resisted the Establishment's embrace. The rest capitulated to the technocratic vision of the planners and bureaucrats. The political and social ethos of popular liberalism, of which Scottish Labour was a part since the time of Hardie, and which the Clydesiders grew up in, was destroyed as a result.

NOTES

1.   E. Shinwell, *Conflict without Malice* (London, 1965), 77.
2.   *Scottish Labour Leaders 1918-1939: a biographical dictionary*, ed. W. Knox, (Edinburgh, 1984), 16.
3.   *Ibid.*, 37.
4.   J. Paton, *Left Turn!* (London, 1936), 145-6.
5.   Knox, *Labour Leaders*, 16.
6.   J. Butt, 'Working Class Housing in Glasgow, 1900-1939', in *Essays in Scottish Labour History*, ed. I. MacDougall (Edinburgh, 1979), 152; R.P. Arnot, *A History of the Scottish Miners from the Earliest Times* (London, 1955), 14.
7.   *New Leader*, 27 December 1941.
8.   Knox, *Labour Leaders*, 53, fn.41.
9.   *Forward*, 12 April 1929.
10.   *Ibid.*, 16 June 1928.
11.   A.L. Drummond and J. Bulloch, *The Church in Late Victorian Scotland, 1874-1900* (Edinburgh, 1978), 145.
12.   W. Knox, *James Maxton* (Manchester, 1987), 37.
13.   *Forward*, 3 April 1926.
14.   Paton, 145-6.
15.   R.E. Dowse, *Left in the Centre* (London, 1966), 93.
16.   *Glasgow Herald*, 17 August 1925.
17.   *Forward*, 28 June 1924.
18.   *Ibid.*, 14 June 1924.
19.   Knox, *Maxton*, 69.
20.   *Ibid.*, 70-1.
21.   NAC, *Minutes*, 30 June 1928.
22.   Knox, *Maxton*, 69.
23.   *Ibid.*, 99.
24.   C. Harvie, *Scotland and Nationalism* (London, 1977), 55.
25.   C. Harvie, 'Labour and Scottish Government: the age of Tom Johnston', *Bulletin of Scottish Politics*, No.2, (1981), 12.
26.   K.O. Morgan, *Keir Hardie: radical and socialist* (London, 1975), 257.
27.   *Forward*, 30 March 1935.
28.   *Election Address*, 1945.
29.   H. Corr and W. Knox, 'Patrick Dollan', in Knox, *Labour Leaders*, 98.
30.   *Glasgow Eastern Standard*, 3 May 1924.
31.   *New Leader*, 24 June 1932.
32.   Knox, *Maxton*, 110-11.

7 INTERNATIONALISM IN THE TWENTIETH CENTURY: SOME COMMENTS ON JOHN MACLEAN[1]

Terry Brotherstone

> The workers have no economic interest ... [in] the war, and because of that, it is my appeal to my class that makes me a patriot so far as my class is concerned, and when I stand true to my class, the working class, in which I was born, it is because my people were swept out of the Highlands. ... I am no traitor to my country. I stand loyal to my country because I stand loyal to the class which creates the wealth throughout the whole of the world.
>
> We are out for life and all that life can give us. I therefore took what action I did in the light of what was transpiring inside Russia, inside Austria, and inside Germany...
>
> John Maclean's speech from the dock,
> Edinburgh, 9 May 1918.[2]

Central to an understanding of the impact of the October Revolution on the 'revolt on the Clyde'—the general title given by William Gallacher[3] to the various manifestations of working-class protest in the west of Scotland during and just after the First World War—must be an assessment of the Marxist revolutionary, John Maclean (1879-1923). Shortly before the Revolution Lenin linked him with Karl Liebknecht and Friedrich Adler as 'the best-known names of the isolated heroes who have taken upon themselves the arduous role of forerunners of the world revolution'. Soon after the Bolsheviks were in power, they appointed Maclean their consul in Glasgow. And when the call was issued, early in 1919, for the founding conference of the Third International, Maclean, alone in Britain, was summoned by name.[4] Yet despite unprecedented attention to him recently in academic work, a strong impression remains amongst many people with a serious interest in Scottish working-class history that John Maclean is either ignored or misrepresented in the history books.[5]

This paradox is of course tied up with the difficulty of arriving at an objective view of the Russian Revolution itself, particularly in its international dimensions. And that difficulty, quite apart from all the usual problems of historical research derives, on the one hand, from the continuing political relevance of the Revolution, and on the other from the distortions its history has suffered in the name of political necessity. The historiography of the subject still inevitably suffers—often in subtle rather than crudely obvious ways—from the influence of capitalist propaganda against the Revolution, or from the grotesque falsifications perpetrated in its name by Stalin and his supporters—of whom, when he wrote *Revolt on the Clyde*, William Gallacher was one.

The best standpoint from which to assess John Maclean's relationship with the Russian Revolution, and indeed his historical significance in general, is 9 May 1918, when he was put on trial in Edinburgh on charges, under the Defence of the Realm Act, of seditious activities. It was the most historic trial that had ever taken place in Scotland, claimed the defendant, because in it the working class and the capitalist class confronted each other face to face.[6] However that claim is assessed, there is no doubt that Maclean's earlier appointment as Soviet consul in Glasgow had played a part in the deliberations of the authorities who decided to proceed with the prosecution.[7] Nor did Maclean enter the trial unprepared. He decided to make no attempt to be acquitted but to rest his 'defence', which he conducted himself, on the rejection of the authority of the court and on a seventy-five minute long speech from the dock, addressed not so much to the judge and jury as to the labour movement in Britain and internationally. It was in this speech that Maclean made the statement printed at the head of this essay in which he connected his parents' experience of the Highland clearances with his own working-class and internationalist loyalties. The remark was surely as much a reference to the role played by the Clearances in Marx's *Capital* (vol.I, chapter 27) as it was autobiographical. It is doubly significant in the present context. The importance of the land question in Scottish radical politics is usually cited in support of the view that there were particular barriers north of the border to the development of a specifically proletarian, anti-*capitalist* consciousness: here Maclean suggests that the intensity of the Highland experience contained the possibility of an opposite effect. And the Clearances—in the memories they left behind at least—were (certainly in the context of Great Britain) a uniquely Scottish aspect of the 'modernisation' process; yet here Maclean cites them as a spur to an internationalist understanding of capitalism as a whole.

Re-reading Maclean's speech today, it is difficult at first sight to understand why it has not had a greater impact on historians. It is logical and well-constructed, a remarkable public justification of his decision to devote his life to educating the working class in Marxist economics, his opposition to the war which he saw as the outcome of capitalist decay, and his support for the Bolshevik Revolution. Its defiant delivery was an act of self-sacrifice which must have been based on a firmly Marxist conviction in the capacity of the working class to overthrow capitalism and create a peaceful world, if only its leaders would show a decisive example. It was a statement based on an internationalism which did not stop at the level of moral principle, but which was rooted in the conception that the working class was an international class, the conception that received its most famous formulation in the *Communist Manifesto* of 1848, and which, for all their ambiguities, had informed the Stuttgart and Berne resolutions on war agreed by the Second International in 1907 and 1912.[8]

Although the trial lasted less than a day, and has left no surviving official transcript, at any rate not in public records open to consultation, it is well documented and clearly created a great interest at the time. The tabloid *Bulletin* daily paper had a picture of well-heeled citizens mingling with workers outside the court, which was so packed that not all who had walked most of the way from Glasgow to attend were able to get in. It also had a picture of Maclean speaking from the dock, the existence of which is something of a mystery, since the taking of photographs in court was, then as now, illegal. In socialist papers—even those opposed to Maclean's revolutionary stand— his actions, and the harsh, five year sentence passed on him, made him a major object of attention. About a month after the trial, Lenin was telling a conference of trade unionists in Moscow that

> the Scottish schoolteacher and trade-unionist Maclean was sentenced for a second time, to five years' imprisonment ... for exposing the real objects of the war and speaking about the criminal nature of British imperialism ... Maclean is in prison [again] because he acted openly as the representative of our government; we have never seen this man ... he has never belonged to our Party, but we joined with him; the Russian and Scottish workers united against the British government in spite of the fact that the latter ... is manoeuvring frantically to drag the Russian Republic into the war.[9]

When Maclean received his first major term of imprisonment, in April 1916, he was initially disappointed at the response in the workers' movement, which, in part at least, was a result of the crisis within his own party, the British Socialist Party.[10] Things changed in the early months of 1917 as opposition to the war mounted and excitement was created by the overthrow of Tsarism in Russia. This period culminated in the famous Leeds convention in June which, however anticlimactic its outcome, represented the strength of the movement for peace and genuine democracy in the working class.[11] The movement for Maclean's release mounted and was eventually successful, despite the (so far as can be judged) sincere professional opinion of some prison doctors that his health would be better served by continued supervision.[12] When Maclean was reincarcerated in 1918, a new situation existed in the socialist movement. The split created by the desertion of the anti-war cause by the parties of the Second International in 1914 and deepened by the Bolshevik Revolution took several years fully to clarify itself; nevertheless it now underlay developments in the labour movement, and there could be no ambiguity that Maclean symbolised the newly defined revolutionary tendency. Yet the solution to the problem of Maclean favoured by the Secretary of State for Scotland on the advice of some doctors—to certify him insane—was dropped; and the possibility that, as a hunger-striker, he might be allowed to die, was ruled out, at least in part for fear of the reaction it might create in the workers' movement.[13] When, following her visit to him in Peterhead jail on 22 October 1918, Mrs Maclean revealed that her husband had been on hunger strike and had been force-fed without her knowledge, the protest movement was so widespread that G.N. Barnes, the coalition Labourite who had replaced Arthur Henderson in the Cabinet, began to press for Maclean's release. Maclean had been chosen as prospective candidate many months before by the Labour Party in Barnes's own constituency, the Gorbals. It may be surmised that the minister feared that he might lose out in the general election likely to be held after the end of the war, if he allowed himself to be identified as one of his opponent's jailers.[14]

It is neither the intention here to reopen the vexed question about the specific possibility of revolution in Britain between 1917 and 1921, nor to suggest that all the attention paid to Maclean was a result of the inspirational qualities of his speech in defence of the Bolshevik Revolution. Throughout 1919 at least, however, Maclean was perceived as a considerable figure, certainly as a propagandist, in the British labour movement; and the relative lack of a record of this in historical accounts of the period must surely be linked with the prevailing assumption underlying the mainstream of English historiography, including labour historiography, that proletarian revolution in the home of parliamentary democracy is, and—despite occasional tremors—always has been, basically unthinkable.[15] In *The Legend of Red Clydeside*, for example, Iain McLean dismisses Maclean's statement in court as follows:

> A study of MacLean's [sic] speech from the dock in 1918 shows that [Secretary of State for Scotland] Munro's assessment of him as 'more or less a lunatic', while exaggerated, was not merely a petulant reference to his political views.[16]

Far from being a balanced judgement on the speech as a whole, this appears rather to be a dismissive opinion based on one section of it; the part of it subheaded, in the pamphlet version which appeared soon after the trial, 'Some British Atrocities'.[17]

It was here that Maclean publicly accused the Peterhead prison doctors of having had his food tampered with during the winter of 1916-17. It was a charge which Maclean was to repeat many times between 1918 and his death, a period of about five years, over a third of which was spent in prison. The authorities were sufficiently sensitive to the accusation to order an internal inquiry, which concluded that it had no substance. A few years ago Gerry Rubin examined the matter concluding that, on the basis of available government records, there was no evidence for Maclean's assertion.[18] Recently further Scottish Office files have become available to researchers. If the point at issue is whether Maclean as an individual had been singled out for drugging, it seems to me that Rubin's judgement is unlikely to be revised.[19]

In my view, however, this is not the point at issue—or certainly not the major one. In the speech from the dock, Maclean was not suggesting that he had been the object of unique attention—although this is the impression left by the extracts quoted by Iain McLean who believes himself to have proved conclusively that Maclean suffered from 'paranoid delusions'.[20] Yet at one point John Maclean specifically stated that

> I saw these men around me in a horrible plight ... I would rather be put to death than condemned to a life sentence at Peterhead. Attacks were made upon

the organs of these men and also upon their nervous system, and we know from the conscientious objectors that the Government have taken their percentage of these men—some have died, some have committed suicide, others have been knocked off their heads, and in this way got into asylums ...[21]

His own treatment in other words was seen as part of the general situation in the prison, whether or not Maclean was wrong in attributing intentional acts designed to harm prisoners' health to particular medical officials.

Far from being evidence of paranoia, the passage on prison conditions has a definite place in the logic of Maclean's speech. He was arguing, in the most practical way, from personal experience, that the prison system was part of the machinery of the capitalist state and that workers and socialists must be warned, as they entered the revolutionary struggles which he saw as being on the immediate agenda, that it would be used ruthlessly against them. Maclean's conception of social revolution, internationalist to the core as he proved by his stand against the war in 1914, his support for the Zimmerwald conference in 1915 and his struggle against the apolitical perspectives of the Clyde Workers' Committee,[22] was based on the idea that leadership was a product of the personal courage and integrity of individuals. It was his responsibility as he saw it to show the working class that—contrary to the appearance of 1914, when illusions in the leaders of European social democracy leading a socialist struggle against the war were shattered almost overnight—the treachery of leaders was not a law of nature. If the very different character of genuinely Marxist leadership could be demonstrated to the working class, through educational work on the one hand, and personal self-sacrifice on the other, revolution, as the crisis of wartorn capitalism deepened, would be assured.[23]

This conception, I think, was adhered to by Maclean until his death. although of course his optimism about the imminence of successful revolution was modified by changing circumstances. This is the thread that runs through his struggle for a general strike in 1919; his attempt to form a Scottish Communist Party in the latter part of 1920; his successful campaign to win a leading role in the Clydeside unemployed movement as the slump took hold; his support for the national struggle in Ireland; his work as a Marxist educator both within and apart from the Scottish Labour College; his continuing— and, contrary to some commentators, far from absurd—analyses and prognostications concerning the economic and political situation; indeed his whole life from his release from prison in early December 1918 until he died prematurely on 30 November 1923.[24] The role played by the theory of encroaching insanity in the historiography of the subject is one of apparently absolving historians, who have difficulty coming to terms with the idea that anyone truly committed to the idea of proletarian revolution in Britain could be quite all there, from the responsibility of seriously examining Maclean's ideas and actions in the last period of his life. The evidence for the theory comes largely from an unimaginative reading of government records, and from the prejudiced reminiscences of William Gallacher.

It is certainly the case that there were prison doctors prepared to certify

Maclean in 1918; but that is scarcely surprising. They were faced with an intransigent, convinced of his own importance, not out of paranoia, but for the political reasons explained above. The medical men were dealing with someone who, in terms of their own social and political outlook, was no doubt inexplicable. They would have used the only concepts they had.

As to Gallacher (whose account Maclean's first biographer, Tom Bell, followed), he had genuinely tried to work politically with Maclean at a very difficult period—particularly during Maclean's candidature *in absentia* for the Gorbals parliamentary seat in the latter part of 1918.[25] The experience had not been a success, perhaps through no fault of Gallacher's. But, however that may be, the political contradictions in which Gallacher was entrapped by the time he wrote *Revolt on the Clyde*, if they did not play tricks with his memory altogether, certainly deprived him of a balanced sense of the significance of things that he did remember.[26] The major question for Gallacher, in this regard, was why he had been unable successfully to carry out Lenin's request that he persuade Maclean to go to the revolutionary Russian republic, if only to recuperate from the strain of his wartime experiences,[27] and presumably also to join the Communist Party. It is not necessary to suppose that the failure of communication was all on Gallacher's side to see that, neither at that time nor later, could he arrive at any theoretical explanation for it. He cannot have been helped, from the standpoint of his own self-esteem, by the public knowledge that Maclean regarded him as a theoretically obtuse semi-anarchist with a negligible grasp of Marxism.[28] In his memoirs, Gallacher got over the problem by recounting tales of Maclean's alleged obsession that he was being pursued by state agents.

By impish quotation from Ramsay Macdonald, Raymond Challinor has demonstrated the absurdity of citing alertness to state penetration of the labour movement at this period as evidence of mental unbalance. A reading of the reports on revolutionary organisations prepared for the Cabinet by Basil Thomson, head of the Special Branch, re-inforces the point. However the reality behind their fears is assessed, leading figures in the state machine *were* fearful of 'Bolshevism' in Britain, and their agents were in the field.[29] Whether Maclean overstressed the danger and became too involved in a form of conspiracy theory which came to view the nascent Communist Party as virtually a creation of the class enemy would be a matter for legitimate debate; although, as with the speech from the dock, it is important to read what Maclean actually said on such questions before dismissing his sometimes one sided conclusions out of hand.[30] What is certain, however, is that for a revolutionary socialist who had been Bolshevik consul in Glasgow to be alert to state surveillance at this period is, of itself, evidence of nothing else but political realism.

What does need much fuller examination is the conception of internationalism that led Maclean to see his presence in Britain in the immediate post-war period as more important than participation in the Third International. Walter Kendall's study of *The Revolutionary Movement in Britain, 1900-21* served, in the late 1960s, to put John Maclean back on the historian's map, but its thesis that the International's concern for the building of a communist party in Britain, as elsewhere, was, by its very nature, subversive of an authentically British revolutionary tradition, may have diverted attention away from an important discussion of the history of internationalism.[31] The use of Maclean's antipathy to the early CPGB as evidence that its very formation was an improper imposition of Russian conceptions inappropriate to a British environment, however attractive the argument may be to adherents of the various doctrines of British exceptionalism, is very much against the spirit of Maclean's own internationalist outlook. Yet it is also the case that Maclean's internationalism did not develop along the lines of that of the Bolsheviks after 1917. When J.D. McDougall, probably deputising for the imprisoned Maclean, and fairly certainly reflecting his views, contributed to a debate in *The Call* in the summer of 1918 on the reconstruction of the International, he did not see it as an urgent task. The 'supreme work', he believed, was 'the education of the masses and their organisation in industry on a Socialist basis, so that they will be able to use their industrial power in politics'. Following the collapse of 1914, the European socialist movement had been 'purified by persecution', and this, he implied, would be sufficient to bring 'the serried ranks of the revolutionary workers' in behind it, as they lined up 'for the next great attack upon Capitalism'.[32]

For Lenin, on the other hand, as Marcel Liebman argues, the old leaders of the Second International would not simply fade away and lose their influence on a militant working class. Their defeat came to be seen more and more—particularly after the victory of October 1917 and the defeat of the German Revolution early in 1919—as a task requiring the establishment of a Bolshevik party on a world scale.[33] Rodgers and Smyth recently argued convincingly against the charge of Tom Bell that Maclean was too much of an individualist and not a party man.[34] But a different point is being made here. It is that Maclean, subjectively a committed Bolshevik, never had the opportunity to study Lenin's conception of the relationship of theory to practice and of the role of a democratic centralist party in establishing the link between Marxist theory and political organisation. He probably never read Lenin's *Left Wing Communism; An Infantile Disorder* and we certainly can never know what he might have made of the struggles which went on for the method underlying it, during the early years of the Third International.[35]

All this, it seems to me, is an essential part of the background to the question of Maclean's perspectives on the Scottish question from late 1919 onwards. These have recently been discussed by Bain, by Howell, and by McHugh and Ripley.[36] The last-named, in particular, went over the evidence on this aspect of things dispassionately, arguing that, whatever the validity or otherwise of the idea of a 'Scottish national question' from a Marxist standpoint 'it was not of primary political importance' to Maclean either in his attempts, in 1920, to set up a Scottish Communist Party, or in his formation, in 1923, of the Scottish Workers' Republican Party. This is not a conclusion palatable to all, but it is to be hoped that the fact that the meaning of Maclean's life is a matter of continuing passionate debate amongst and between Scottish nationalists and socialists today will not lead to scholarly abstention from an issue so clearly related to contemporary politics. The disputes about Maclean which periodically erupt in the Scottish newspapers— and not only the left-wing weeklies—are, in any event, evidence that he is considered worth fighting over in the context of rival, but living, traditions of revolt.

There is much more arguing to do about John Maclean; and more work to be done. Unlike some figures from 'Red Clydeside', interest in him is never likely to be purely academic, nor confined to those content with orthodox ideas about parliamentary history. In some accounts of the Clydeside revolt it can seem as though it is being consigned to the 'if only' school of history. If only John Wheatley, the catholic socialist who was a successful housing minister in the 1924 Labour government, had lived. ... If only Tom Johnston, the indefatigable journalist and later corporatist Secretary of State for Scotland in the Second World War coalition, had been more charismatic. ... If only the inspirational Jimmy Maxton had been less ineffectual. ... John Maclean does not lend himself to 'if onlys' based on orthodox historiography. But his life does seem meaningful in the context of a revolutionary tradition which, contrary to what is often implied, does have its place in Scottish labour history.

The record of Maclean's struggle, and of the considerable response to him in the working class which helped sustain it, is above all, it seems to me, evidence of a tradition of Marxist internationalism in recent British history. To sustain this argument it is important to challenge apparently authoritative assessments of Maclean's alleged paranoia and general mental instability. And labour historians, if they are now beginning to pay real attention to Maclean, cannot be permitted to compartmentalise his historical role as being primarily that of a 'passionate [Scottish] nationalist'.[37] There is room for discussion about Maclean's latter-day views on the Scottish question. But his central significance in Scottish—and in British—history lies in his inter-nationalist stand against the First World War, his capacity to evoke a quite remarkable interest in Marxist economics amongst Scottish workers, and his practical support for the Bolshevik Revolution. If these things could be dis-missed as the actions of a madman it would certainly remove a whole range of complexity from the enterprise of explaining the evolution of contemporary Scotland. But the truth is seldom as simple as conventional thinking would like to make it.

NOTES

1. This piece is an abridged and amended version of a 'discussion article' which appeared in the *Journal of the Scottish Labour History Society (JSLHS)*, 23 (1988), 15-29; this issue of *JSLHS* is substantially devoted to the impact of the Russian Revolution on Scotland. I am grateful to the editorial collective for their agreement that I should use this material here. I should also like to thank Hilary Horrocks for her critical assistance with this contribution and the one that follows. Nothing in either should be blamed on her however.

2. For the most complete reprint of the original pamphlet containing John Maclean's speech from the dock, see *Accuser of Capitalism: John Maclean's Speech from the dock* ed. T. Brotherstone (London, 1986). There is a regrettable number of misprints, but they are mainly obvious. The quotation is at *ibid.*, 31.

3. William Gallacher, *Revolt on the Clyde* (London, 1936).

4. V.I. Lenin, *Collected Works (CW)* (Moscow, 1960-), XXVI, 74; Nan Milton, *John Maclean* (London, 1973), 155ff.; *Documents of the Communist International* ed. Jane Degras (London, 1956), I, 4.

5. I base this observation in part on remarks made at the three annual John Maclean Memorial Lectures which have been held since 1986. See my discussion article, *JSLHS* (1988), 27, notes 1 and 3; for recent work on Maclean see references in notes 29, 34, 36 and 37 below.

6. In addition to the edition cited above, the speech from the dock is available in Nan Milton, *John Maclean: In the Rapids of Revolution* (London, 1978), 100-14.

7. Brotherstone, *Accuser...*, 9-12.

8. For the Stuttgart resolution, see James Joll, *The Second International 1889-1914* (London, 1955), 196-98.

9. Lenin, *CW*, XXVII, 483.

10. John Broom, *John Maclean* (Loanhead, 1973), 85.

11. On the Leeds convention see, for example, Raymond Challinor, *The Origins of British Bolshevism* (London, 1977), 180-83.

12. Scottish Record Office (SRO), HH 16/123 (14 June 1917).

13. e.g. SRO, HH 16/125 (May-July, 1918).

14. SRO, HH 16/134 (November-December 1918); Barnes had also taken up Maclean's case, as an MP, in 1916-17.

15. Making fun of 'historians treading the infertile deserts of British labour history in a search of a revolution manquee' (G.A. Phillips) is a not unpopular sport. See Henry Pelling, *Popular Politics and Society in Late Victorian Britain* (2nd edn., 1979), viii.

16. Iain S. McLean, *The Legend of Red Clydeside* (Edinburgh, 1983), 145.

17. Brotherstone, *Accuser...*, 25-7.

18. Gerry Rubin, 'A Note on the Scottish Office Reaction to John Maclean's Drugging Allegations...', *JSLHS*, 14 (1980), 40-5.

19. SRO, HH 16/122-137, *passim*. When Maclean was on hunger strike in 1918, however, the possibility that he might be permitted to die was aired, as stated above; but that course was not followed.

20. McLean, 'Letter', in *History Workshop Journal (HWJ)*, 20 (1985), 22.

21. Brotherstone, *Accuser...*, 26.

22. Milton, *Rapids*, 76-7, 84-5, 91-3, etc.

23. Maclean's classes in Marxist economics from about 1908 until his death are reviewed and discussed in the biographies by Milton, Broom and elsewhere. In 1919, according to one of Special Branch chief, Basil Thomson's, spies, his

conception of the force of sacrificial example was such that he thought he was 'more good to the cause in prison than out'. PRO, CAB 24/74, GT 6713 (28 January 1919).

24. For the issues raised here, though not necessarily support for the analysis, Broom, *John Maclean*, caps. X-XIV; Milton, *John Maclean*, caps. XLIII-LXVI.

25. SRO, HH 16/123 has material casting light on this.

26. Gallacher, *Revolt...*, esp. 213-16. See also his *Last Memoirs* (London, 1966).

27. Gallacher, *Revolt...*, 214.

28. J. Maclean, 'Open Letter to Lenin', *The Socialist*, 30 January 1921; and other writings of Maclean at this time, some of which are reprinted in Milton, *Rapids...*, 224ff.

29. R. Challinor, 'John Maclean', *HWJ*, 22 (1986), 220-21; PRO, CAB 24/91 indexes the Thomson reports for 1919; the working of the far from excitable mind of Walter Long on the question of Bolshevism is documented in Phillip Knightley, *The Second Oldest Profession* (London, 1986, Pan paperback, 1987), 56-7; for other sources see, for example, Challinor, *Origins...*, cap. IX; Christopher Andrew, *Secret Service* (London, 1985), esp. cap. 7.

30. Milton, *Rapids...*, 224-29, for example.

31. Walter Kendall, *The Revolutionary Movement in Britain, 1900-21* (London, 1969), part 2, *passim*.

32. *The Call*, 8 August 1918.

33. Marcel Liebman, *Leninism Under Lenin* (London, 1975), esp. 385ff.

34. M. Rodgers and J. Smyth, 'John Maclean: Organiser for the Socialist Revolution', *Radical Scotland*, December/January, 1984, 20-2. This brief but valuable article deserves greater notice and debate. It makes some particularly interesting comments on the relationship between Peter Petroff (for whom, see *Scottish Labour Leaders 1919-1939*, 224-30, entry by Rodgers and Smyth) and John Maclean.

35. On the debates in the early years of the Communist International see, for example, *Proceedings of the Second Congress of the Communist International* tr. R.A. Archer (London, 1977), *The Communist International in Lenin's Time* ed. John Riddell (New York, multi-volumed publication in progress, 1984-), *Theses, Resolutions and Manifestos of the First Four Congresses of the Third International* ed. Bertil Hessel (London, 1980).

36. Graham Bain, *John Maclean: his life and work 1919-1923* (Glasgow, n.d., 1986?); David Howell, *A Lost Left* (Manchester, 1986), esp. 203-25; J. McHugh and B.J. Ripley, 'John Maclean, the Scottish Workers Republican Party and Scottish Nationalism', *JSLHS*, 18 (1983), 43-7.

37. Rightly or wrongly, this is the impression left by Howell's essay on Maclean on reviewer David Rubinstein: see *Society for the Study of Labour History Bulletin*, 52 (1) (1987), 82.

8 IN LIEU OF A CONCLUSION

Terry Brotherstone

The short essay making some points about the significance of John Maclean was added to the seminar papers which form the core of this book in order to balance its treatment of the nineteenth and twentieth centuries with that of the seventeenth and eighteenth. John Brims raised issues concerning the years when the French Revolution dominated politics in Scotland; it was, therefore, appropriate to round off our examination of aspects of the history of the working-class movement by asking some questions about the impact of internationalism in the period when the Russian Revolution influenced perspectives. Prompting questions is what I hope this volume has been about. Of the six main essays, each I am sure will have won particular admirers; but it is on the book as a whole that I want to comment briefly here.

It has argued no collective thesis, nor has it been the result of a well financed and systematic project. It is rather the product of a modest and exploratory exercise. Its subtitle—'Traditions of Revolt and Protest in Modern Scotttish History'—refers to what the original seminar series was called; and has been retained because the three concepts of the title were all to play a part in organising subsequent struggles, or legitimising them in the consciousness of participants. It implies no claim to elaborate a theory of tradition, no strict definition of revolt and protest, no aspiration to comprehensiveness. Readers will want to draw their own conclusions as to the value of juxtaposing analyses of events from the last four centuries in this way.

Three things however encourage me to think that this volume, despite its lack of a particular 'line' or authoritative conclusion, may be relevant to at least some participants in the current debate about Scotland, and to those whose lives will be affected by its outcome. The first is the nature of that 'debate' itself. The second is the current state of Scottish historiography. The third is the character of the Aberdeen seminars which have given rise to the book. I shall say a word or two about each.

'We are making history', declared chairperson Canon Kenyon Wright to the first meeting of the Convention to demand a Scottish legislative assembly, held in the Church of Scotland's Assembly Hall in Edinburgh on 30 March 1989. Not so, the abstaining Scottish National party and the hostile Conservatives declared by their absence—at least as official bodies. The SNP's rejection of the Scottish Convention, at least at that stage, was of especial significance in the light of its dramatic re-entry into the mainstream of Scottish politics at the Glasgow Govan by-election of 10 November 1988, when its candidate, Jim Sillars, had overturned a previous Labour majority of over 19,500 to win comfortably. Whether or not this event gains an important place in history remains to be seen; but it encouraged speculation at least. Could it be that a new conjuncture of circumstance and tradition might be producing a challenge to the established parliamentary order such as that signalled on Clydeside at the general election of 1922? If so, how should that conjuncture be understood? What factors, combining the international, the British, the Scottish and the local—and what meeting up of historical tradition with current problems and perceptions—had created it? And if Govan was not just another in a spasmodic series of by-election upsets which have punctuated electoral history since the Labour and Conservative parties occupied the two ends of the see-saw of parliamentary politics, if it really did reflect some underlying turning point, how could a class-based electoral revolt—for Govan was clearly a predominantly working-class constituency—be expressing itself through support for the Scottish National Party? Leftward-leaning the SNP might legitimately claim to be, but it was also based on a capitalist programme and the idea of a unity of interest of all classes in Scotland.[1]

If there was a sense of history about the Govan result—and it was not only the understandably enthusiastic Nationalists who thought perhaps there was—what was its relationship to Canon Kenyon Wright's claim to be 'making history' at the Scottish Convention? As an ecumenical methodist he was perhaps impressed that such an apparently secular and broadbased campaign should have been launched in the Assembly Hall of the Church of Scotland. Clearly, however, he meant something more than that; although, in passing, it may be observed that, if there was to be the possibility of a revolt of the Scots three and a half centuries after the Covenants, the episcopate was no candidate to be made the unifying scapegoat. To many it seemed that Mrs Margaret Thatcher, leader of three radical Tory governments since 1979, which lacked much evidence of electoral endorsement in Scotland, was bent on adopting that role for herself.

The point for us about the relationship between the Scottish Convention and Govan is that the special interest in the Scottish question in the late 1980s lay precisely in the combination of constitutional and class questions which it involved. The language of the particular movement behind the Convention helped to suggest this. The document which gave rise to it was the Campaign for a Scottish Assembly's *A Claim of Right for Scotland*, published in July 1988.[2] Its title referred principally to the document submitted to William III and Mary in 1689 by the Scots nobility detailing their conditions of allegiance. Its imagery therefore suggested it was opening up questions which the revolutions of the seventeenth century—the basis on which the Union of 1707 was concluded—were supposed to have settled. The Union of 1707, and the 'Glorious Revolution' of 1688, it was being implied, had not after all secured the individual liberties of the Scottish people; had not therefore provided a fundamental basis for the accomplishment of the political demands of the bourgeois revolution.

This interpretation is supported by the close ties between *A Claim of Right for Scotland* and Charter 88, a British-wide movement launched late in November 1988 which also demanded constitutional review.[3] It was remarkable not so much for its complaints against the Thatcher governments' attacks on civil liberties, which others were also making,[4] as for the historical nature of its charge that these attacks were made possible by the 'dark side' of the traditionally much admired constitutional settlement of 1688-89 itself. It also specifically objected to the fact that, in its view, 'Scotland is governed like a province from Whitehall'. The title *A Claim of Right* had alluded mainly to the seventeenth century, but also to an attempt by the Church of Scotland to maintain its unity in the early 1840s. This latter *Claim* was made to a Westminster government thought by the church to be insensitive to its particular role in bourgeois Scotland in the period when it faced the social problems to which chartism gave political expression. Charter 88 clearly took its title from chartism itself, from the People's Charter of 1838; but also from Charter 77, the movement for 'human rights' established in Czechoslovakia in 1977. The suggestion here was that, while horrendous denials of individual liberty had been carried out in the twentieth century by rulers claiming to act in the name of the proletariat, western regimes in general, and the British government in particular, should consider the abuses of the basic rights supposed to be secure in capitalist society rather than indulge in triumphalist preaching at eastern Europe.

'The Scottish question', then, arose in the late 1980s in a very different way from the rather routine and often confusing 1970s discussions about a measure of legislative devolution which had ended with the referendum of 1979 and the subsequent fall of the Labour government. On the one hand it was part of an international discussion concerning individual human rights and national or regional self-determination. This latter aspect found a particular focus in the idea that, if the European Community became more politically centralised in the 1990s, it would require to recognise autonomous regional institutions not necessarily tied to existing nation states. On the other hand, a central issue which would have to be faced by the constitutionalists who were campaigning for a Scottish assembly was whether such a body could alleviate social problems, such as those of the Govan working class, sufficiently to ensure that episodic electoral and other protests did not turn into serious revolt. This was perhaps what that infuriatingly allusive 'newspaper', *The Economist*, meant when, in an article on 6 May 1989 backing devolution against the policy of the Thatcher regime it normally supported, it observed:

> The recent Scottish 'constitutional convention', dedicated to discovering a formula for home rule, is the polite version of sentiments normally expressed more rudely.

I am not suggesting that historical study will itself answer 'the Scottish question', which, in my view, is in reality a number of separate but related questions; only that, along with economic and sociological analysis, it is an essential component in determining the nature of the period we are in—and, therefore, what sort of answers should be sought.

This leads to my second point 'in lieu of a conclusion'. Whoever looks for historical knowledge to illuminate her or his perception of 'the Scottish question' today is beginning to be much better served by the writing available on the subject. Much research remains to be done of course. But just as important at this stage is how the results of existent and future research begin to inform the consciousness of those in Scotland today who are coming on to the scene to make their own history; which means, I am quite sure, not just to debate and rationally plan the future, but to identify the real alternatives and, in one way or another, to fight them through. Scottish history-writing cannot in itself be expected to play a direct role in this, since there is no obligation on historians to prescribe political answers, and they sometimes write bad history when they try to do so.[5] Nevertheless Scottish history as a field of study has changed significantly in the last quarter-century, and not only in the number of books and articles produced. The point is best made by three quotations. In 1970 the Tudor constitutional historian, G.R. Elton, remarked:

> The Scots, it is said, love their history but do not study it— perhaps love it the more easily because they do not permit study to interfere with preconceptions.[6]

But in 1988 in an 'English Perspective' on the study of the history of Scottish social development between 1500 and 1800, K.E. Wrightson remarked:

> We have much to learn from those of the current generation of Scottish historians who have sought to overcome a marginalisation of their national past too readily conceded by some of their predecessors, by adopting a consciously comparative strategy of historical research and interpretation.[7]

And John Dwyer has recently suggested that:

> It is both refreshing and revealing to discover that, at the same time as English history is becoming increasingly insular and particular, its Scottish counterpart is busy exploring connections, developing comparisons and contributing to an understanding of the modern world and its ideological divisions.[8]

It now seems possible to claim that, without surrendering its standards—indeed arguably because of the raising of its standards—Scottish history is ceasing to be the remote and conservative field of study it was not so long ago perceived to be. It is becoming much more relevant to a general understanding of Scottish society on the one hand, and, in its own particular way, world history on the other.

At the Aberdeen seminars, however, questions were put which suggest this process is still in a transitional, and perhaps precarious stage. The discussions which took place involved historians of Scotland, other historians practising in Aberdeen, and non-historians. Some of the matters raised—particularly the relationship between past and present and between empirical work and interpretative disputation—are reflected in the points already made. But perhaps the main concern centred on the need for Scottish historians to engage *more* in discussion of international comparisons and influences, and in more explicit dialogue with historians of other parts of the world working in Scotland. Was Scotland so very different from other societies in the seventeenth century? How important was international Calvinism to the Covenant, and the European experience of Scots mercenaries to the success of the covenanters? Are we yet clear about the impact of the French Revolution on the radical movement in Scotland? In what relationship did Scottish chartism stand not only to the British movement of which it was a part but also to the emergent European revolutions of 1848? Can the lack of political success of the Clydesiders be fully understood outside of a general analysis of the crisis of European social democracy after 1914? These were only some of the questions raised.[9]

Recent trends—as reflected in Dwyer's remark especially—suggest that to call for a more international perspective on Scottish history is to knock at an open door. But the point is worth stressing nonetheless. And, even if the essays in this book themselves concentrate mainly on exclusively Scottish matters, it is to be hoped that its general approach and the sort of dialogue promoted in the seminars might provide an example which could contribute to the door being thrown wide open. What is involved is not simply producing ever increasing numbers of monographs of a standard that may convince Professor Elton that some Scottish historians are fit to sit at High Table with their English peers. It is ensuring that Scottish historical interpretation—based on, and interrelating with, serious research—enters unequivocally into the mainstream of the interpretative disputation which, however much many historians today seem temperamentally disinclined to admit it, has always been a vital driving force in the promotion of a better understanding of the past in general, and European history since the seventeenth century in particular.

These comments have been devoted mainly to suggesting some questions and possibilities which, it seems important to me, should be pursued further. But on one matter I imagine I can speak for all the contributors. The exploration of at least some aspects of revolt and protest has proved to be a productive and stimulating exercise; and further work along these lines should have a very definite part to play in the developing process of establishing what are the essential trends in modern Scottish history. One possible line of approach has been briefly indicated by David Stevenson, a participant in the seminars, in a chapter of his accessible study of *The Covenanters*. He points out that their inspirational legacy was long-lived, but that the two major periods of covenanting history provided alternative images in a more recent period for movements with different class bases. Insofar as the covenanters were an inspiration to participants in working-class movements it

> was the later covenanters of the Restoration period... but it was the years of Covenanting rule after 1638 and the attempts then made to protect Scotland's

identity within Britain through a new federal union that had most to offer
patriotic movements: the Covenants not as symbols of class conflicts within
Scotland but on the contrary as standing for the unifying of men of all ranks
in patriotic struggle.[10]

Covenants, albeit of a limited and agnostic sort, were indeed launched by
Scottish nationalist or Home Rule movements in the 1930s; and in the late
1940s the then Scottish Convention's Covenant was claimed to have over
two million signatures. It was, however, purely a protest movement which
petered out as post-war recovery began to bring some material benefits in the
1950s.[11] As Stevenson also indicates, the Covenants had less anodyne echoes
in the twentieth century for opponents of a united Ireland who claimed to be
defending the Protestant constitution established under William of Orange.
On 13 May 1989 the memorial to the covenanting martyrs in Edinburgh's
Grassmarket was the symbolic starting point for some aggressive young men
seeking to disrupt a much postponed and heavily policed demonstration by
the Republican Bands Alliance in commemoration of James Connolly (1868-
1916) whose birthplace is less than a hundred yards away in the Cowgate.
Connolly, the trade union organiser and socialist republican shot by the
British authorities following his part in the 1916 Easter Rising in Dublin, had
been an associate of some of those who became the 'Red Clydesiders'. The
1989 clash in Edinburgh between orange and green was a minor affair, but
it served as a reminder of why covenanting images could not provide an
unambiguous message for those seeking electoral support for their attempt
to take the red flag to parliament.

If further work on what the Covenants meant to subsequent protest movements might be illuminating, the same is true of chartist studies, in which
reconstructing the historical record and determining the meaning of the
struggle for the Charter for succeeding generations have always been closely
connected. In both cases historians are obliged to confront contradictory
traditions, reflecting at the same time changing circumstances and the contradictions within the original events themselves. There is no single undis-
puted heritage. Introducing John Maclean into the discussion about the
Clydesiders helped to show that this also applies to the concept of a working-
class party. The idea that such an organisation was the necessary instrument
of working-class opposition was adumbrated in the period of chartism. It was
given reality in many countries in the last third of the nineteenth century,
and, although Britain had to await the dawn of the twentieth century for its
Labour Party, the Scottish Labour Party, founded in 1888, was one of its
harbingers. The collapse of the declared internationalism of European social
democracy in face of the First World War and the Bolshevik Revolution,
threw into turmoil complacent ideas about the nature of such parties. John
Maclean never joined the British section of the Third International—the
Communist Party of Great Britain—and that organisation was soon to
degenerate into a notoriously pliable instrument of the whims of Stalin.
Nonetheless the recorded wrestlings of Maclean, William Gallacher and others

with the issues involved in the aftermath of 1917 serve to place such questions on the agenda of Scottish history.[12]

Another approach could be to follow up the work of the Clydesider who later became Secretary of State for Scotland, and later still Chancellor of the University of Aberdeen, Tom Johnston. In his radical days, when the ILP was preparing its assault on Westminster, he perceived a need for combining scholarship and popular presentation in studies of, amongst much else, the covenanters, radicalism and chartism. The result was published in 1920 as *The History of the Working Classes in Scotland*, having previously been serialised in Johnston's *Forward* newspaper, whose sales it did a great deal to boost.[13] Johnston's biographer, while paying tribute to the 'formidable ... historical endeavour' and 'prodigious research and meticulous attention to detail' which went into the book, adjudges it 'first and foremost ... a propaganda tool'.[14] The point is more profound than might appear at first sight, since it revolves around a critique not so much of the use of historical scholarship for political purposes, as of the theory of the development of socialist consciousness underlying the politics of the ILP. For the propagandist the essential weapon in the struggle for socialism was to show the people the true facts so that they could use their democratic power to bring about socialism. Maybe the naiveté underlying that conception helps to account for the fact that Johnston's history is today almost certainly more read by older labour movement activists than by young people or historians. Yet however old fashioned Johnston's politics may seem, his challenge as a radical writer of history has never been fully met—neither by friend nor foe of his basic historical propositions.

When the third edition of his book came out in 1929, Johnston regretted he had not had time to do more work on it, but claimed 'there is nothing to withdraw' since 'the historical pundits and apologists for the existing order of society' had

> failed ... to find anything upon which to base a charge of inaccuracy in fact or of error in interpretation.

If, he continued

> the slaveries, robberies, murders, class cruelties, and oppressions be proven ... then the greater part of the drum and trumpet history and ruling caste ancestor worship with which our children ... are primed, would appear to be ever more ridiculous and irrelevant.
>
> It is an abiding and indisputable truth that a people which does not understand the past will never comprehend the present nor mould the future....[15]

Johnston saw his essays on the history of the working classes as a contribution to such an understanding. It was a worthy aim. Today, six decades of political experience and a quarter of a century of intensive research in modern Scottish history provide us with advantages Johnston lacked. Yet 'drum and trumpet history' is far from dead—even if it now tends to make its entrances in more sophisticated garb. If the present volume were to make even a modest contribution to encouraging others to advance Johnston's declared purpose on the basis, not only of greater knowledge, but also of creative criticism of his method, it would, in the editor's personal view, have been well worth the effort.

NOTES

1. A reporter for *The Scotsman* (11 November 1988) characterised Sillars himself as:

   > very much an operator within the capitalist system—he is chief executive of a Glasgow exports firm—[who] clearly sees himself as a radical Left-winger, and believes other members of his party would benefit by cleaving to the same mould.

2. *A Claim of Right for Scotland* (Edinburgh, 1988) was published as the 'Report of the Constitutional Sterring Committee' presented to the Campaign for a Scottish Assembly; it referred to two previous Scots' initiatives 'against misgovernment' under the same title, that presented to William and Mary in 1689, and that presented to parliament by the Church of Scotland in 1842. In 1989 it was reprinted with commentaries in a book with the same title edited by O. Dudley Edwards.

3. For Charter 88, see *New Statesman and Society*, 2 December 1988, 10-11. It rejected 'the complacency with which the tercentenary of 1688 has been celebrated'; reasserted 'a tradition of demands for constitutional rights in Britain' going back to Magna Carta in 1215 and including 'the working men who drew up the People's Charter in 1838' and 'the women... who demanded universal suffrage'; and also referred to 'the Czech and Slovak signatories of Charter 77 on human rights. Writing in support of Charter 88, Anthony Barnett claimed: 'Along with the sustained and detailed *A Claim of Right for Scotland*, Charter 88 points towards a new kind of politics in Britain' (*Ibid.*, 14). On the day of the first meeting of the Scottish Convention—30 March 1989—the occasion was greeted by the Charter 88 supporters with a full page republication of their document in *The Scotsman*.

4. See, for example, Peter Thornton, *Decade of Decline: Civil Liberties in the Thatcher years* (National Council for Civil Liberties, London, 1989), which accused the government of producing 'almost a state of peacetime emergency' (*ibid.*, 91).

5. For a recent, serious but in my view not entirely successful attempt to summarise Scottish history from the standpoint of present-day socialist revolt, see Mick Hume and Derek Owen, *Is there a Scottish Solution? The working class and the Assembly debate* (London, 1988).

6. G.R. Elton, *Modern Historians on British History 1485-1945: a critical bibliography* (London, 1970), 198. Elton immediately conceded that there was 'less truth in this opinion than once there was', but still recorded 'a disappointingly small' number of writings of the standard 'of professional work commonplace in English and Welsh history'. This sort of work had 'become at all prominent in the northern kingdom' only during the previous decade, he asserted. And while his strictures against the general inadequacy of Scottish history-writing could not 'be at all applied to Smout's very fine social history of early-modern Scotland [T.C. Smout, *A History of the Scottish People, 1560-1830* (London, 1969)], a well-planned, sensible and fascinating work ...', Elton noted that this book, which ought to 'have been regarded as good and most welcome, was in this case received with extremes of rejoicing or disapprobation, provoked by the destruction of comfortable legends ...'

7. K.E. Wrightson, 'An English Perspective', in *Scottish Society 1500-1800*, ed. R.A. Houston and I.D. Whyte (Cambridge, 1989), 259.

8. John Dwyer, 'Prospero's Mantle: Recent Trends in Scottish History', *Scotia*, (1988), 55.

9. Amongst other points discussed was the possibility that latter-day influences of the Covenant might include the attempt to make the world 'safe for democracy' after the First World War; since Woodrow 'Wilson gloried in the Scottish presbyterians' fight for religious liberty and was fond of evoking the picture of the signing of the Covenant on a tombstone in Greyfriars Church in Edinburgh'. On 18 December 1918, in London, as US President, he declared, 'The stern Covenanter tradition that is behind me sends many an echo down the years'. Eleven months earlier Wilson called in his '14 Points' for 'open covenants of peace openly arrived at'. Edwin A. Weinstein, *Woodrow Wilson: a medical and psychological biography* (Princeton, 1981), 6, 317. I am grateful to Professor Paul Dukes for this reference.

10. David Stevenson, *The Covenanters* (Edinburgh, 1988), 70-84.

11. For an account of these movements, see for example J. Brand, *The National Movement in Scotland* (London, 1978).

12. For Gallacher's debates with the Bolshevik leaders on these questions, see especially *The Second Congress of the Communist International*, tr. R.A. Archer (London, 1977), II, 42-4, 167-69, 181-88.

13. Thomas Johnston, *The History of the Working Classes in Scotland* (Glasgow, 1920); T. Brotherstone, 'The Suppression of the "Forward"', *Journal of the Scottish Labour History Society* (1969), I, 8.

14. Graham Walker, *Thomas Johnston* (Manchester, 1988), 47.

15. Johnston, *op.cit.* (3rd edn., Glasgow, 1929), 5. Johnston's time was evidently even more at a premium between 1929 and the publiction of the fourth edition in 1946. In the latter, even the 'prefatory note', although now dated 'May 1946' is almost word for word what it was in the third edition. A photographic reprint of the fourth edition was published by EP Publishing (Wakefield) in 1974.

INDEX

This index is indicative rather than exhaustive. The names of contemporary authors are included only if they appear in the main text, or if a footnote contains substantial information.